LEST WE FORGET

Lest We Forget

A POW Memoir of World War II

DAN M^cCULLEN

FITHIAN PRESS · SANTA BARBARA, 1997

Published by Fithian Press
A division of Daniel and Daniel, Publishers, Inc.
Post Office Box 1525
Santa Barbara, CA 93102

Book design: Eric Larson

LIBRARY OF CONGRESS CATALOGING-IN-PUBLICATION DATA
McCullen, Dan, (date)
    Lest we forget : a POW memoir of World War II / by Dan McCullen
        p. cm.
    ISBN 1-56474-191-5
    1. McCullen, Dan. 2. World War, 1939–1945—Prisoners and prisons,
German.   3. World War, 1939–1945—Personal narratives, American.
    4. Prisoners of war—United States—Biography.
    I. Title.
    D805.G3M428   1997
    940.54'7243—dc20   96-20479
                                                                CIP

To my wife, Beth Rathell McCullen,
who patiently listened when I needed to relate past
experiences but could not do so because of emotions, and
who encouraged me to record these experiences for our
daughters as part of their heritage.

And to my daughters, Dane, Lyn, Dale, and Jill,
in order that they will know something of their heritage
and realize that the freedoms we enjoy are the result of
much sacrifice and prayer during bygone days.

ACKNOWLEDGEMENT

An acknowledgement and a debt of gratitude is owed to my next-door neighbor, Mrs. Fannie Virden McGehee, who read an early version of this manuscript more than twelve years ago. At that time, my memoir was in the form of a letter to my daughters, and after reading the unfinished product she wrote:

"It seems to me that this journal rightfully is, first of all, a very moving piece of writing, important in its original purpose as a legacy to his little girls, and to all who know and love him.

"It is also much more than this. It is intensely interesting, observant, and thoughtful, transcending the factual reporting of one segment of our history, which, like all good writing, becomes instructive, revealing, and inspiring.... Dan's answer to all that happened, his strengthened faith, his awareness that everything in life, the good and the bad, should be used for development by growing closer to God, makes a solemn, even sacred legacy to his family and his friends."

"Miss Fannie" now refers to me affectionately as "her boyfriend," and I to her as "my girlfriend," all with my wife, Beth's, approval. While living next to me, she continued to encourage me on a regular basis to pursue the publication of my memoir. She now resides in a retirement home, but on each occasion that Beth and I visit with her or converse by telephone, she wants to know the status of the book and what we are doing to have it published. It was she who put me in touch with Fithian Press, and were it not for her persistence, my memoir might still be gathering dust in a closet. I saw her on her 100th birthday party and she commented, "Dan, don't be too long getting the book published."

CONTENTS

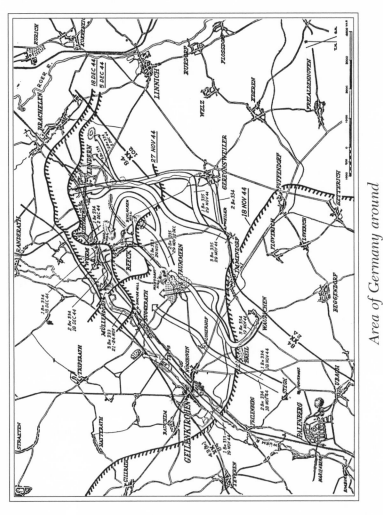

Area of Germany around
Geilenkirchen, Müllendorf, Suggerath,
and other locations mentioned in the text

PROLOGUE

ALL THINGS
WORK TOGETHER

"And we know that all things work together for
good to them that love God." Romans 8:28

WHAT I WANT TO RELATE now is an experience I had
which was so overwhelming that it has been foremost in my
mind for over forty years. It is difficult to understand what
goes on within us and about us, and yet there is no question in my own mind that everything is planned.

It is upon this premise, then, that I believe I have to be
one of the most blessed individuals there is or has ever
been. I feel that I am proof positive that there is a blessing
in everything.

The more I ponder over how this tale should be unrav-
eled, the more I realize that I will have to bare my soul, as
I cannot relate this story without exposing my relationship
to God.

The One Upstairs allowed me to endure an experience
more than forty-five years ago as a German prisoner of war.
Little did I realize at the time that I was being richly
blessed. I prayed and talked with Him on a daily basis,
wondering why He was permitting such an ordeal to occur.
As I reflect back on those years now, I realize that He has
taught me to appreciate what He did for me. Little did I

realize at the time that He was putting me through a test. Indeed, He was tempering my metal for the life which lay ahead. I was more richly blessed than anyone I know, and I failed to comprehend it at the time.

It is difficult to comprehend an experience so awesome and so overwhelming that it becomes your constant companion. Not a day passes that my thoughts do not reflect back to those days in Germany. Not a night passes that I do not feel some physical or emotional symptom of it. Few meals have I eaten without my reflecting on those days when there was no meal. How often in Germany I was aware that I could have lived handsomely on the scraps from my mother's table.

I believe that there is a blessing in even the darkest hour, if you look for it and work at it. It may be the darkest hour and the conditions may be unbearable; yet it may be your brightest hour. I sense that I am a living example of the truth of this.

LEST WE FORGET

CHAPTER I

PREPARATION

THIS MEMOIR BEGINS in the fall of 1942. That was the beginning of a series of events which ultimately led to my getting to the eye of my needle in Germany. I was a fuzzy-faced nineteen-year-old beginning my junior year in pre-med at Millsaps College. The war was going pretty strong, but the draft age had not yet been lowered to nineteen. My friends were either volunteering or attempting to get into some type of reserve program which would permit continuation of their education. Unfortunately, due to my undeveloped left eye, I was not able to do either. I went to the recruiting offices for all services in the downtown post office building during October 1942, but I could not pass the physical for any service. The officers in charge simply advised me to return to school and perhaps the draft would not bother me.

During the latter part of November 1942, however, the draft age was lowered to nineteen, and this necessitated my registering. My left eye afforded no hindrance at all to the draft, and on December 24, 1942, I received my notice to report for induction at Camp Shelby, Mississippi, on January 6, 1943. Thus, on a cold, gray day in January, 1943, I was sworn into Uncle Sam's Army, but on limited service. This meant that I was supposedly unfit for overseas duty and unfit for combat, and this was stamped on my service record. We were given one week in which to put our home affairs in shape, and on January 13, 1943, I was fitted with my first suit of Uncle Sam's olive drab. Because of my limited service status, I received no basic training, normally a thirteen-week course, which included close order drill, weapons, military courtesy, and what have you.

At first, I spent three months at Camp Shelby in pre-induction classification. Lieutenant Ray Musgrave was instrumental in placing me on his team. He had been professor of psychology at Millsaps College, and our function was to give pictorial aptitude tests to prospective inductees who could not read or write but who might have some background or talent which could be utilized by the Army. It was while conducting these tests that I became aware of the appalling illiteracy among the inductees, both white and black, from Mississippi. Regardless of illiteracy, we did induct both blacks and whites who possessed skills—such as truck driving, carpentry, mechanics and other trades—which could offer some assistance to the military.

In March 1943, I was transferred to Camp Murphy, Florida, which was a radar school. I was placed in intelligence there, as there was a need for screening all new inductees coming into Murphy because of the high secrecy of radar at that time. Purser Hewitt, who was a Jackson sports writer for the *Clarion-Ledger*, was a lieutenant there and second in command of the intelligence office (under Captain White), and it was Lieutenant Hewitt who arranged for me to be placed in intelligence while at Camp Murphy. I spent one month in the Everglades before joining his office, however, as a part of a detail which had to construct tent cities around Lake Okeechobee to house natives from the Bahamas who were to be shipped in to harvest the foodstuffs which abound in that fertile peat soil.

During the summer of 1943, the colleges and universities had been so depleted of students that the Army Specialized Training Program (ASTP) was started. This was available to Army personnel who had made a qualifying score on an IQ test and who had some college background. It was necessary to take an additional IQ test to qualify for the program, and I was fortunate to be accepted and transferred to Virginia Polytechnic Institute in Blacksburg, Virginia, during September 1943. In my mind, I feel that this program was designed to help keep some of the colleges and universities open and, at the same time, maintain a reservoir of available troops.

I was very fortunate to be able to complete two college semesters in engineering at Virginia Polytechnic Institute before I was transferred to the Railsplitter Division at Camp Claiborne, Louisiana, in March 1944. These credits could be transferred to Millsaps and they ultimately allowed me to finish Millsaps within a year after my return.

Army life was very frustrating, however. I grew quite restless and was not satisfied with what I was doing. I had been turned down for Officer Candidate School (OCS) because of my left eye, and most of my Army activity had become pretty boring. Whether fortunately or unfortunately, Mother kept all of my letters, and there is a thread of boredom and frustration running through the lot. My group apparently lived from one rumor to another, never knowing what the order of the day would be. I suppose we were frustrated at Blacksburg because we were put back into an academic life, and none of us felt that we were really contributing to the war effort. I had been in an academic atmosphere of my own choosing at the time of my draft and I resented having been uprooted from my home environment for the war effort and then being thrown back into the classroom hundreds of miles from home. We felt that we were just marking time while at Blacksburg.

Virginia Polytechnic Institute was a military school and

the community of Blacksburg welcomed us with open arms. Nevertheless, my letters, even from Blacksburg, suggested a restless and frustrated Dan McCullen. I guess that I had the vim and vigor of youth and the dreams of youth and the Army interruption had not been a part of my plans.

On November 14, 1943, while at Blacksburg, I wrote Mother that I had definitely changed since my induction, but whether the change was for better or for worse I did not know.

We had had a discussion in class that day on what the war was all about and what America should ask for after the war. Most of the class felt that we should become a sort of imperialistic nation to police the whole world; for some reason, I took the opposite approach and felt that there should be some disarmament, although a certain amount of policing would be necessary. Then, in my letter to Mother, I said:

> There will have to be disarmament, and we will have to have more teachers and missions than we ever had. The church is going to have to have a bigger hand in the peace than it did last time. These things seem to be inevitable.
>
> I am in a state of evolution and what finally evolves, I won't know.

I felt that within me were two personalities. One, the outer, which I showed in my daily life, and the other, my innermost thoughts, which were my own beliefs and convictions. Although I was a practical joker, I had a serious side of which few were aware. Looking back on my thoughts of myself at that time, it seems a little strange that I would be mentioning the role of the church in our country's future. Yet, in the same letter, I discussed

Mississippi's liquor problem (a dry state) and revealed to my mother, "a teetotaler," that I had had beer the previous Saturday.

Strange that I should write my mother that I had had a beer, knowing what a fanatic that she was against it.

In reflecting back over three decades and in reviewing some of my thoughts as a twenty year old, I realize that the present young generation probably is not any more uppity than was my generation. Although the letter reflects a tone of loneliness and frustration, I obviously felt that if I put my mind to thinking on a particular problem that I could come up with some solution. There were worlds to conquer and accomplishments to be achieved, and I was so frustrated because the Army was causing a delay. I was dreaming the dream of youth. Little did I realize that what happened day by day was adding an element of experience to which I could cling at some future date. Each little bit combines to make the whole, and without the frustrations and delays and the ups and downs, you do not learn how to appreciate the good things which happen. To me, every experience, then, is a part of an overall plan, and your success or failure to a large extent depends on your reaction to these experiences. From my experiences, I am increasingly convinced that it is not our plan but His plan, and each bitter frustration is a blessing in disguise.

I have always had a deep respect for my family and my country, and I am thankful that my parents exposed me to the church at an early age. Many were the Sunday mornings, however, when I did not want to get dressed to go to Sunday School and church. Although I was exposed to the church at an early age, I never did become a fervent activist who wanted to thrust my religion on another. I had my own deep feelings, which were private. I could be obstreperous and rebellious and insubordinate, and I am sure that mother agonized about me. I did heed her early training, however, and kept in touch with the church, although at times it was irregular. Fortunately, there was a First Christian Church in Blacksburg, with Reverend Eubanks as pastor, and I attended regularly, much to the delight of my mother.

My pastor at home was Dr. Bert R. Johnson, with the First Christian Church, and my family had attended his church since arriving in Jackson in the summer of 1938. He and I corresponded on a limited basis, and he gave one of my letters to my mother for safekeeping. This letter was written just two days before I turned twenty-one:

Saturday, 2:00
Dear Dr. Johnson:

I certainly did appreciate your last letter so much. I am sorry to be so long in answering, but it seems that my time this semester is even more occupied than last semester.

Yet, I am just two days from being 21. Truly, it seems only a step; I can remember vividly many instances of early childhood even before I started to school. Yet, when I enumerate past experiences, there seem to be so many. All have meant something to me. The ups and downs have all fitted into a pattern that makes life so real, so enjoyable. I have had a great time. I have grown to love people, to enjoy doing things, and to enjoy and to understand a few of the manifold experiences of nature. I owe all that I have gained to the home from which I came. I only hope that I can live up to the ideals set for me by my parents.

It is true we know not what lies ahead, but each little experience will mean the building of a stronger character. The world, itself, is in a great turmoil today. Judging from all of the reports we hear each day, I have every reason to believe that I will be sailing by fall. This is alarming, of course, but it is as it should be. I am thankful that I am able to participate if the need calls for it. I will go with an open mind and an open heart, knowing that in some small way it will be for the good of all.

Dr. Johnson, my furlough seems as if it were ages ago. I am sorry that I did not get to see you. Maybe before many moons it can be arranged.

Sincerely,

Dan

It seems that in the Army we just lived from one rumor until the next. At that point, little did I realize that in March the entire cadre of personnel at VPI would join ASTP troops from several other universities to become a part of the 84th Division at Camp Claiborne, Louisiana. Here I became a part of the infantry, still with "limited service," "unfit for overseas" and "unfit for combat" boldly printed on the outside of my service record. I had not yet had basic training when I was issued an M-1 rifle at Claiborne. Fortunately, I had been raised in the outdoors of Mississippi, and I was able to conform to the infantry routine, although not without some misgivings. The 84th had been in training probably for a year, and it was composed of a lot of its initial recruits. It had trained at Camp Howze, Texas, and it had been on maneuvers and it wound up in Camp Claiborne. Although we had people from all forty-eight states, a large portion was from the southwest, including Indians, Mexicans and Spanish Americans. Some of the older members in the division taught me how to break down a rifle, and I soon was able to take it apart and clean it and put it back together blindfolded. The ASTP group was given thirty days' provisional training before joining regular companies, and this thirty days' training was all that I had by way of basic training. It was during this training that I was thrown with Bill Long of Quincy, Illinois, and he and I became foxhole buddies for all of our training in Louisiana.

Although Bill and I both attended VPI, we were in different dormitories and we did not know each other. The first time that I recall meeting Bill was during our first bivouac in the wilds of Louisiana. This was during our thirty-day training period and late one afternoon the cold rains commenced. Each soldier had to choose a buddy as each carried only one shelter half, and the two halves had to be buttoned together to make a tent. Fate thus threw Bill and me together to fashion hurriedly a tent to protect us from the elements. We must have looked like Mutt and Jeff; I was five feet nine inches tall, and Bill had to be at least six feet three inches.

We threw that first tent on a side of a slight incline and the waters seemed to flow right through the middle of our tent. We used our mess gear for pillows and I seriously doubt that we slept a full hour that night. It was experiences such as this, however, which made us fast and steady friends to this day.

After our thirty days' provisional training, we became a permanent part of the 1st Platoon, Company L, 333rd Infantry Regiment. We had field problems with the division for several weeks through July 1944. Infantry training in the sand and piney woods of south Louisiana during the hot, humid summer months was certainly no bed of roses. I learned to fire the bazookas and the rifle grenades; just a few from each platoon did. All were taught the use of the rifle and hand grenades. At some point in mid-summer, I was transferred to the BAR (Browning Automatic Rifle) team. This was something of a demotion in that the BAR weighed twenty-three pounds, and it was my constant companion on the four-, nine- and twenty-five-mile hikes. Again, I had no special training in the BAR and others had to teach me what I learned about it.

In spite of the training routine, we developed a very close-knit group, and I made some very fast and lasting friends among our group. Despite the frustrations of training routine, we were able to maintain a strong morale because of our youth and frivolity. Although my letters reveal a continuing tone of frustration and disgust with the Army, I was enjoying my friendship with my new comrades. I suppose we were a pretty bad lot to get along with. I was still being obstreperous and a little insubordinate when I thought the occasion called for it. While at VPI, there were, of course, no advances in grade, and I was still a buck private after a year and one half in service. In fact, it took about that long before I was awarded the good conduct medal.

Our group took particular delight in needling Corporal Cornelius Abraham of Lafayette, Louisiana. Cornelius was a Louisiana Frenchman from crawfish country, and he spoke his English with a Cajun accent. On one particular field problem, we were in the cut-over piney woods embarking on a little field maneuver for the night. Cornelius was explaining the overall problem and he prefaced his remarks by stating, "This is east," pointing to the east, and "this is west," pointing to the west. I remarked, "Gee, this must be north," to which Cornelius said, "I don't know, they didn't tell me that."

I probably also caused no end of consternation to Lieutenant John Guerry of Chattanooga. John, then better known as "Red" Guerry, was a shave-tail lieutenant, just out

of military school and OCS and a couple of years the junior
of me and most of the other boys in the platoon. I suppose
I was still rankled for having been turned down for OCS
because of my left eye, only to wind up in a combat infantry division. In any event, we had to stand inspection every
Saturday morning, and the main targets were the condition
of your rifle and your dress code. When I finally made private first class, rather than sewing my stripes on my sleeve,
I simply took a pin and pinned them on, and Red Guerry
was about as rankled with this tactic as was I for having
been turned down for Officer Candidate School.

On another Saturday morning, Lieutenant Guerry was
inspecting my rifle for rust and upon close look, he said:
"McCullen, I believe I see a spot of rust in your chamber."
To which I replied, "No sir, I believe that's a reflection
from your hair." This, of course, did not set too well with
the redheaded lieutenant.

On another occasion, we were out in the field and I had
done something to irk the lieutenant. He drew off a square
under a pine tree and said, "McCullen, dig a foxhole here."
Well, I had dug more than my share of foxholes, since I
was paired with Bill Long, and he was six-feet-three and
you had to dig each hole deep enough to take care of the
tallest in the crew. I therefore had dug about one half foot
more foxhole on each occasion than should have been required of me at my height. In any event, the lieutenant left
after giving me instructions to dig the foxhole, and I
scooped about two inches off the surface of the ground,
just removing the grass, and I let it go at that. About two
hours later, the lieutenant came by and I snapped to attention and gave a smart salute, standing at a height equal to
his and looking eyeball to eyeball. He promptly inquired:
"McCullen, where is your foxhole?" To which I replied: "I
am standing in it, sir."

In spite of our many antics like this, we became a very close-knit team.

Rumors were still a great part of the action, and we did not know what the future held. In May we were told to get our legal affairs in order and to designate place of burial. All of the men in the division were given furloughs during the summer of 1944, and the disabled who would not qualify for overseas or combat were transferred. Fifteen men were transferred out of our company on July 5, 1944, and it appeared that we were nearing the time that we would be headed overseas.

On July 25, 1944, Colonel Tandy Barrett of Tuscaloosa, Alabama, advised us that no furloughs would be granted after August 15, 1944. We were issued brand-new rifles and combat jackets and we were also given airborne training with gliders and C-47 cargo planes. Rumors started flying then that we would probably head for Burma as its only access was by air.

I did not know Colonel Barrett personally in 1944, as my only contact with him at Camp Claiborne was from some distant pine stump when he would try to impart words of wisdom to the troops gathered. On one such occasion he admonished us to get with the training for our own protection. His words, although a little saltier, in effect stated that we had better do our training properly now, because once we got in combat, we were going to be shaking like a birddog passing peach seeds. Colonel Barrett and his lovely wife have become my very close friends during recent years and to show you how small this world is, he is a member of Uncle Charles' church in Tuscaloosa.

Mother, of course, was very upset with the thought of me going overseas, but my letters to her during the summer of 1944 reflected an eagerness on my part to get on with it and to go overseas. Maybe this eagerness was brought about by my desire to get out of the Camp Claiborne environment.

We left Claiborne in late August or early September and went to Camp Kilmer, New Jersey, which was the port of embarkation (POE) for New York City. We were stationed at Camp Kilmer for about two weeks, as we had some last minute training and medical tests to pass. There was a series of shots that each of us had to take and we had to have some last minute training on climbing up and down rope ladders on the side of a ship. Training was not intense and most men were granted liberal one-day leaves of absence to tour New York City. We couldn't afford many trips on our pay as most of us had allotted deductions from our check to go to our families. Although the money was short, we had a ball when we were able to get to the Big Apple. I was able to get a USO ticket to a Broadway comedy, which was a real treat.

On September 19, 1944, we sailed in a large convoy along the southern Atlantic route, arriving in Scotland on or about October 1, 1944. We then traveled by rail through Glasgow, Scotland, south to London and to a camp near Newbury. After we left the States our mail was censored and its arrival unsure. Mother and I numbered each letter in the hopes that we could keep up with those which were lost. I was in England only one month. Actually we were not scheduled to go to England in the first place. We were to have landed at Cherbourg, France, but that port got messed up, and we wound up with a delightful month in England, although the weather was wretched. A letter written on October 7 described some of my impressions of England.

Saturday
October 7
Dear Mother:

I suppose you have been anxiously awaiting some news other than a hello note. I have been rather uncomfortably situated up until now, but everything is now under control. Plumbing and lights make all the difference in the world, when you have to give them up for a while.

Mother, I will try to cover as much as possible what I have seen and done since I left the States. The last phrase seems kind of odd, doesn't it—back in the States. I was wondering for a time whether or not I would even get across. That was always my desire when I got in the Army. I probably will become dissatisfied here after a time, but now, while everything is new, I don't think I will mind it. It won't do any good to think otherwise now anyway. I wish now more than ever that I had called you before I left, but toward the last it was impossible for me to get a call through. My first letter was written before we debarked, but it did not contain anything. The trip as a whole was very pleasant. We had movies, books, boxing, and music as entertainment on board, and there was either one or the other in process at all times. Of course the most enjoyable thing I encountered was the amount of sleep. I practically slept my way across. I also ran into K.P. enough that I did not get hungry.

Everything seems different to me here. Of course, this is war country, and it has been hit hard by the war, but the people, the customs, the styles, and the cities all seem to be back a few years as compared to the States. The industrial section looks most

like that of ours, I believe. The cities have old buildings, and the architecture is only of one type. The
shops appear dark and dingy and there is not too
much night life. Of course, the people are still under
the influence of blackouts in some sections. Everyone seems to be very busy all of the time. They appear to be very conservative. The big difference is
that they don't shun the soldiers. Everyone rushes to
their window and waves a V for victory. It isn't like
the States where you are looked down on the minute
you hit town. This has been interrupted. Will write
when possible.

    Love,
    Dan

My rebellious nature was still manifesting itself in
southern England, and when it was necessary for a two-
man detail from our platoon to be selected for a menial
chore in Dorchester, it was Ralph B. "Squeak" Williams
and I. To show you the way the Army is, they took me off
the BAR team on the boat and made me second scout. This
meant that I was teamed up as a foxhole buddy with
"Squeak" Williams from Idaho, and this to some extent
separated me from Bill Long, who remained on the BAR
team. In any event, it was necessary that Squeak and I pre-
pare barracks for the arrival of a new division to be quartered in Dorchester in southern England. A large number
of troops had been quartered here prior to their commitment on D-Day. The Dorchester assignment was supposed
to have been a punishment of sorts for something that
Squeak and I had done which peeved Lieutenant Red
Guerry. Our feelings were not so strong, however, that I
had any reluctance about going to the lieutenant to see if
he had any money that I could borrow for that week's trip.

Unfortunately, he had none, as all of us had left just about all of our paychecks for allotments to our families.

When Squeak and I got to Dorchester, we found that we were unassigned; we were able to eat at the Headquarters' Company mess hall at any time, and we had no duties to perform. We spent a week having a lark on the town, and it so happened that this was the home town of Thomas Hardy, the British novelist. Although we were pretty certain that we were headed for combat and knew not what the future held, I spent as much time as I could learning what I could. I apparently was cocky or confident enough to believe that, whatever the future held, somehow I would make it all right and return home.

While I was in England during October 1944, there were a lot of rumors that the European war would be over during the fall of 1944. I even wrote in one letter that our unit would perhaps become occupation troops. It had been anticipated that the parachute drop on Arnhem, Holland, in September 1944, would probably do Hitler in. It was known in October that the mission at Arnhem had failed. This was the valiant effort by elite troops from England, Canada, Australia and the United States to parachute into Arnhem and then circumvent the northern edge of the Siegfried Line. They anticipated entering German soil without having to make a frontal assault on the mighty Siegfried Line, which Hitler had constructed to defend the integrity of the West German border. This mission failed, however, in September, and is the subject of a recent book entitled *A Bridge Too Far*. I was fortunate enough to associate with some of these British soldiers when I later arrived at Stalag XIB.

Although I was writing to Mother as if I would be a part of occupation troops, our training as a combat outfit was ongoing during our stay in England. The British newspapers were publishing nothing but the European fracas and they concentrated principally upon the action of their own units. Little could be gleaned of American action in Europe and nothing was ever written about the Pacific engagement with the Japanese. This is just human nature, however, as there is nothing so important as your own little world.

We were finishing up our tour in England at the end of October, as all of the 84th Division was to be reunited as a unit in France during early November 1944. My last letter from England was dated October 29, 1944, and I told mother that the next time that she would hear from me I would be in the haunts of Mr. Coullet. Mr. Coullet was a native of France and he and his wife taught music and language at both Millsaps College and Belhaven College. Mother was aware of his background, and this was my means of letting her know approximately where I would be. Letters were censored and I was not sure that I could tell her that I was in France. Everyone seemed to develop some sort of code to let the home front know what was going on.

We crossed the English Channel on the last day of October, 1944, and we boarded LST boats on the French Coast and landed at Omaha Beach, the site of the D-Day onslaught, on November 1, 1944.

During the next several days, we marched inland by day and bivouacked at night in the French apple orchards. Winter was upon us with sleet, snow and freezing rain. War and mud must go hand in hand.

My letters home were becoming less frequent. For several days, we trudged through the mud of France, and we slept in sleeping bags without taking time to pitch a tent. It had become so cold that I mentioned in one letter that it would likely be a one-bath winter.

After trudging through France on foot for several days, we joined the Red Ball Express, the allied trucking unit which ran around the clock, moving troops and supplies to the front. We then boarded open G.I. trucks, and we hurriedly passed through the edge of Paris, Belgium, and into Holland. We arrived in Holland around November 9, 1944, and we were billeted in a Catholic monastery at Gerleen, Holland. Gerleen was just across from the German border and its mighty Siegfried Line. We continued with some of our training while at the monastery, but we were housed inside where we could remain warm and dry and this gave us opportunity to catch up on some of our letter writing. On Sunday, November 12, 1944, I wrote to Mother as follows:

Pfc. Dan M. McCullen, 34614910
Company L, 333rd Infantry A.P.O. 84
c/o Postmaster, New York, New York

No. 27 Sunday
November 12, 1944
Dear Mother,
    I have been busy today catching up on correspondence. I sent out about a half dozen Christmas cards that I purchased in Andover, England. I also sent a pamphlet to you about the cathedral at Winchester. I mentioned it once before. It is one of the largest in Europe.
    When I was in France and Belgium, I saw many things of interest. I only wish I could tell you about them, but I suppose we can wait for a while. I don't believe any country has suffered as the papers try to make you believe. Our propaganda agents can make you believe most anything. The biggest need I be-

lieve is clothes. Most of the clothing was scanty, and wooden shoes seemed to be fashionable. There seemed to be quite a bit of livestock present, and farming seems to be going on in its own way. The beasts of burden seem to be oxen, donkeys and large work horses. A large portion is done by hand. The wagons are merely two-wheeled carts.

For some reason, I feel more at home in Belgium or Holland than France. France, however, is much more extensive and was largely agricultural. The smaller countries were probably harder pressed by the Germans, for there seems to be a concentration of industry in the two. Nevertheless, wherever we go we receive a warm welcome. The people are really grateful to us, and would part with the shirt on their back, if they thought we wanted it. I have seen some of the cutest kids imaginable. I can't resist throwing my gum and candy to them. I wish I had enough for them all. They give us apples and souvenirs of all sorts.

I have about written out for one day. I got to church this morning. When you see a group of men here in church service with weapons in hand, you can't help but notice the grim, determined expression of all present. It is really touching.

Mother, rest assured that whatever I undertake over here, I go by His light. I am happy, contented, and unafraid, so please don't worry. Should anything happen here, I wish you would drop a line to Brother A.H. Eubanks, Blacksburg, for me.

Good night and sweet dreams.

Love to all,

Dan Buck

Although my former letters had suggested we might become occupation troops, there was no escaping the fact that the war was still being waged and the Germans were feverishly defending their fatherland. The Siegfried Line had already been attacked a few miles south at Aachen, and we were poised just a few miles west of Geilenkirchen, Germany, just waiting for orders to commit us to commence the attack on the Siegfried Line at that point. There was not any doubt in my mind that we were headed for combat in a big way within a matter of days.

The letter which I wrote to Mother on November 12 was the last that Mother would receive from me before she was notified that I was "missing in action." The Lord had to help put the last paragraph of that letter in place so that Mother would know that I was in His hands and for her not to worry. Mother received the November 12 letter on December 6, and that was her last contact from me until late February 1945, when she learned by a card from me that I was a prisoner of the Germans. I am sure she clasped that last letter close to her bosom and read and re-read it as her glimmer of hope.

Although I wrote many letters, there was an obvious break in the sequence and some were lost. Also, I remember distinctly writing some letters for the benefit of my censors. The letters were being censored by the officers in our company and largely by Lieutenant Red Guerry with my platoon and by Lieutenant Coakley with the 2nd Platoon. I was certain some of my letters would not pass censor, but I feel they accomplished some purpose. I recall vividly that Lieutenant Guerry called me aside for a little heart-to-heart talk while we were at the monastery in Gerleen, and he wanted to know if anything was troubling me. Man, I had troubles galore, for they were still trying to teach some of these fellows how to fire the rifle grenade while we were on the brink of combat. The lieutenant wanted me to carry rifle grenades in my ammo bag after they had moved me to the scouting position. I simply told him that I was not going to carry those heavy rifle grenades, because my position as scout was to be far out in front, and I would not have been close to the grenade launcher. And here I was on the brink of combat, classified as limited service and unfit for overseas or combat or OCS training.

As foreboding as things were, however, it was a great satisfaction and a great feeling to know that I was going to be able to do my own thing and not have someone do it for me. In fact, my right side had bothered me so that I had trouble on the twenty-five-mile hikes when I carried the BAR; when at Gerleen, Lieutenant Guerry was solicitous of my condition and even offered to have me transferred. I would not have thought of transferring at that time, since I had trained with those fellows to do a job, and I was going to see it through. I could not have stood myself if I had transferred at that point.

CAMP CLAIBORNE, 1944

Standing: Howard Hyle, Robert Rachofsky,
William Long, John Guerry
Kneeling: Vince Loguidice, K. Gregory Tarpinian

William A. Chantry; Berion Smith; William J. Long;
Vincent J. Loguidice; Ralph B. (Squeak) Williams.

Top:
Dan McCullen

Middle:
Ernest "Chief" Stanley

Bottom:
Bob Rochofsky

Mail call at Camp Claiborne
Standing: Paul Ferdinandsen; Ernest "Chief" Stanley; Robert
H. Stott; Robert C. Rachofsky; unknown; Robert Reed
Kneeling: Howard Hyle; Steve Krupa; mail clerk (unknown);
Dan McCullen; William Chantry

Below: Standing: Dan McCullen; William J. Long; William
G. McClain; Howard H. Hyle;
Kneeling: Vincent J. Loguidice; William Chantry

CHAPTER II

THE BATTLE

I AM SURE that our field grade officers were furnished detailed intelligence of the terrain we were to attack and the overall goal to be accomplished. How much of this intelligence trickled down to our company and platoon officers is unknown. Being an enlisted man, I can attest that precious little information was furnished us except that we knew we were going to be hitting the Germans on their home soil and in the thick of the mighty Siegfried Line. The Ninth Army Operations IV, *Offensive in November*, now declassified, described the task as follows:

> The 84th Infantry Division lost little time getting into combat. Division Field Order No. 1, dated 4 November at the Normandy bivouac area, directed movement to Ninth Army's area, which was completed 10 November. The division attitude was summed up by General Bolling:
>
> "Upon arrival in Holland instructions were issued and it was learned that we had been selected to break the Geilenkirchen stronghold. Those of the staff who fully realized the importance of this assignment joined with me in feeling highly complimented that the division should be selected for such a mission inasmuch as it had been the policy heretofore to break in new divisions solely by

placing them in the line where they were subject to hostile fire prior to being given a unit mission."

While the 84th Division was controlled operationally by British XXX Corps in the Geilenkirchen phase, it remained under XIII Corps for administration, evacuation and supply.

The Würm River is the only terrain feature distinguishing the landscape in the area under consideration from that already described on the XIX Corps front as flat with open fields, close set hamlets, mines and slagpiles. Normally the Würm is 16 to 33 feet wide, 2½ to 5 feet deep, with a moderate current. It flows northeastward through Geilenkirchen, joining the Roer depression 10 kilometers north and three kilometers east of the town.

Geilenkirchen is within the borders of Germany, a dot in the dragon-toothed Siegfried Line. It was a market town, a rail and road center. Civilians had been evacuated some weeks before the attack and the interval devoted to frantic community digging. Steel and reinforced defensive structures abounded.

Aerial photos showed southwest of Geilenkirchen, nine pillboxes, 12 concrete shelters, two concrete shelters with cupolas, and an antitank wall consisting of rectangular 5" by 5" steel posts approximately 3-1/2 feet high, spaced 10 inches apart and embedded in a concrete base. This barrier ran in irregular lines parallel with the Würm River, between the river and the Palenberg-Geilenkirchen railroad track. Its length was approximately 2,000 yards. The pillboxes here were similar to those in the Siegfried installations.

Geilenkirchen was not suspected to be a fortress city of the Siegfried Line and this was ultimately proved correct. Pillboxes were not found in the community itself.

(Enemy Fortifications) Northeast of Geilenkirchen to Suggerath (885655) the fortifications increased in number and variety; 17 pillboxes and eight concrete shelters were located in the 1,800-yard interval. Between the two towns at 875644 was a concrete shelter built inside a harmless looking old brick barn. Pillboxes in haystacks, minefields, fire trenches and machine gun pits were not rare. In Suggerath proper two pillboxes were found in shells of brick buildings.

The villages of Müllendorf (901667), Würm (908672), and Beeck (910662) were well outposted with pillboxes, minefields and trenches. The natural approach to Beeck is over open, flat country. Along the Würm River Valley a rolling hill (905657) with seven pillboxes and interconnecting fire trenches protected the gateway to Würm.

Prummern, 2,000 yards east of Geilenkirchen, is in a small valley that becomes deeper to the northeast until at a point about 300 yards from Prummern, in the same direction, the ground rises again to form a plateau to Beeck.

The enemy took advantage of the only possible avenue of approach over this exposed terrain and constructed his pillboxes accordingly. Photo interpretation showed several of them in draws where our infantry normally would not expect to find them. The one at 883641 is an example.

All pillboxes in the area were connected with fire trenches. This system had been so well prepared that it was possible for a soldier to leave his pillbox at 883641 and, by utilizing these trenches

and a slight defilade, reach Prummern without exposing himself to normal observation. Nine pillboxes, six weapon pits, numerous fire trench systems and antitank ditches running just south of the
road Immendorf to Geilenkirchen were reported.
Community diggings were plentiful.

A characteristic feature of all German villages,
in this sector, which readily lends itself to defense,
is the formidable basement which exists in practically every building. These spacious basements are
divided into compartments or rooms. The ceiling,
or first floor, is usually reinforced with I beams, a
feature which nullifies the effect of artillery fire.
Windows can usually be employed as firing aper-
tures. If the enemy makes a determined stand in a
village each individual basement requires the attention of attacking troops and the process of digging
him out may be difficult.

The enemy placed his pillboxes and shelters on
this key terrain. He prepared reverse slopes as well
as forward slopes with foxholes and cut natural tank
approaches with numerous antitank ditches. His
prepared concrete shelters and pillboxes reinforced
by communication and fire trenches, made the
Geilenkirchen area formidable.

(Plan of Attack) "The advance up the Würm
River Valley," stated [Division Commander Major
General Alexander] Bolling, "was a most difficult
operation for new troops inasmuch as the entire
valley was covered by the Siegfried defenses. That it
was the most likely avenue of approach to the main
Siegfried Line was well known to the enemy when
he established these defenses. It was therefore decided to envelop the likely avenue of approach and

take the high ground that dominated the Würm Valley."

Much of the foregoing information was obtained after the fact, as these operations were not written up until the skies cleared and the blood had dried.

On Friday afternoon, November 17, we moved by truck into western Germany. Our mission was to attack the Siegfried Line along the Würm River from Geilenkirchen through Suggerath and Prummern and on into Müllendorf and Würm. On that Friday night, the air was cold and crisp and clear. The large blue search lights focused on the skies, much as seen at our State Fair. A part of our platoon was able to get in an old masonry building, and we took turns standing guard, giving the others a chance for catnaps. The next morning we moved into the apple orchards just out-side Geilenkirchen, and there we dug our first foxhole to be prepared for artillery or attack. British tank units were assigned for our armored support, and on the 18th, we were simply in a position of hold, waiting for the British on the north and the 334th Infantry Regiment of our division on the south to secure the high ground on either side of Geilenkirchen. We were assigned to Simpson's 9th Army.

Sunday morning, November 19, was the day of our commitment to attack. We were to receive one last hot meal, which was breakfast. This, incidentally, was the last hot meal which I would have prepared by an American un-til late June 1945. Little did I realize this, however, at the time. I shall never forget that the first serving in that chow line was hot rum or brandy for those who wanted it. We were under British command and rum is a regular part of the daily ration. I did not partake of the rum or brandy, but those who did had to accept it in their coffee cup—a part of the mess gear. They would have to consume it on an empty stomach before reaching the end of the line, because the same cup had to be used for the coffee. I can still remember one fellow passing through for the brandy on several occasions for the purpose of bolstering his morale. He had the reputation during training of being the great fighter. Some had said that when we got to combat that he would be hell on wheels. He was to conquer the enemy single-handed, they thought. It turned out that when it became time to face up, he was not able to keep muster. I suppose that it was in times such as those that the metal in one's spine either shined or melted, and his melted.

After that last hot breakfast, we embarked on the attack of Geilenkirchen. At that point, our platoon was not the lead platoon in the assault. Geilenkirchen was in the Würm River Valley and appeared to be in the middle of the Siegfried Line with its pillboxes and tank traps. My directions escape me now, but we had to be attacking in an easterly direction at what must have been the southern portion of Geilenkirchen. Aachen had been the first large German city to feel the brunt of the American attack and Geilenkirchen was the second. The fall of 1944 would be the first time ever that American troops fought on German soil, and it would be the first time in around 200 years that British soldiers fought on German soil.

Toward dusk, our units had made it through the southern edge of Geilenkirchen, and we were directed to proceed east toward Prummern and Suggerath. We got into the western edge of Suggerath, and houses and buildings were on fire from the artillery blasts and some may have been deliberately set by the German army.

From our squad, Squeak Williams and I were dispatched to go through a series of houses to clear out any Germans who may have been there. About all that we could go through were the cellars, because the upper structures

were on fire for the most part. It was then decided that our
company would be dispatched eastward along the railroad
tracks to the eastern side of the village of Suggerath. While
the weather had been cold and clear a day or so before, it
had become quite foreboding and wet. Squeak and I were
leading two columns of our company down a ravine beside
the railroad tracks, and as we approached the eastern edge
of Suggerath, we were met by small arms fire, almost point
blank. We hit the ground and then scrambled on our bellies
over the adjacent hillside and dug in for the night. Lieutenant Red Guerry crawled from hole to hole to check on our
deployment and to see that everything was all right. Squeak
and I were in our own foxhole.

It seems that we dug all night. The weather was horrible, and we tried to dig out a cave so that we would get
some protection from the cold rain. One of us would maintain a vigil for the enemy while the other dug. Then, after
we had the hole deep enough, one at a time would catnap.
A foot soldier's life was such that he could sleep almost in a
standing position. During training, I could sleep during the
ten-minute break with nothing but a helmet for a pillow.
Needless to say, little sleep was experienced by anyone in
our group on the night of November 19, as the enemy was
all around us.

At daylight, we surrounded a rural home just on the
eastern outskirts of Suggerath, and Squeak and I started
into that cellar just as we had other homes the night before. For some reason, I grabbed Squeak halfway down the
stairs and told him to back out. I then dropped a grenade
down the stairs and out came nine Germans, including two
SS troopers. Only one German was wounded by the grenade. At this point, the German eighty-eights (artillery)
came in and we were able to get shelter under a railroad
trestle, but then snipers started taking potshots. It was nec-

essary to do a cleanup job back behind us then and we spent most of that day in and around Suggerath in a cleanup effort.

About midday, our platoon got caught in an artillery barrage, and Squeak and I were already down about a foot with our foxhole when Colonel Tandy Barrett came by and told us to get the hell out of there. We then went up the side of a hill where there was an abandoned pillbox, and all hell broke loose. On that hillside, we apparently were visible to the Germans manning the eighty-eights, and, on top of that, we found ourselves in the middle of a minefield. One boy apparently was hit in the pit of the stomach by the eighty-eight; all that remained were his legs. We were supposed to have been issued arctic boots to protect our feet from the mud, but only those people wearing size six shoe or less were lucky enough to get arctics. That victim was to be identified by process of elimination; he had such small feet that he had on arctic boots.

I found myself behind a building and in a slight recession in the side of a hill. The eighty-eights were still coming fast and furious, and one came so close that it almost shaved me. It was about this time that Lieutenant Red Guerry caught shrapnel in his leg. I got to him and tried to help him, but he ordered me into the pillbox, and he awaited the aid of a medic who was nearby. Guerry, of course, was relieved because of wounds, and I was not to see him again until a visit to Chattanooga some thirty years later. We spent the night of the 20th in this pillbox, but it was necessary for patrols to work out of the pillbox all night. These normally were five-man patrols, and I can only remember that it fell to the lot of Squeak and me from our squad to go on patrol. Who else was with us, I do not know. We had to make our way through a certain part of the village to be sure that the Germans had not reinfiltrated. We did not have a "front" such as that portrayed by the old World War I movies. Everything was very fluid and our patrol would have to walk up and down the streets silhouetted by all of the fires which were still blazing in the buildings. It was almost as though the mission of the patrol was to draw fire to determine where the enemy was. You never knew which steps would be your last. As we worked our way back to the pillbox, we still had the worry of having to cross the mine field which surrounded the pillbox. It was in the middle of this mine field that Lieutenant Red Guerry caught the shrapnel from the eighty-eight that same afternoon.

Throughout these combat days, my thoughts were forever on home and my relation to God. In fact, as I recall, I tried to repeat the Lord's Prayer to myself almost as if it were an incessant chant. When you are in that position and all hell is breaking loose, you have to question God's purpose. If He is a loving and compassionate God, why would He permit a holocaust such as we were then experiencing? Some things can't be explained, but having experienced it, I know now that He was making me a little tougher for things to come. In this sense, then, I was being blessed in a way I did not realize. I continued to repeat His prayer and to ask Him to hold my hand, and no one will ever know how closely He held me. Any step could have been my last, and yet He walked with me and protected me. On one occasion, Squeak, a few others and I hid out in one cellar which was an ammo dump. One shell burst in that dump would have blown up a block. We left that cellar and within minutes after we left it, it was blown to bits. This is just an example of fate. Squeak and I were never five yards apart for all of this period and on one occasion a mortar shell fell right between us but it did not go off. Why, we didn't know. Looking back, it just seems as if we were saved by one miracle after another. The week before in Gerleen, we had been told to look on either side of us, because the following week, there would only be one of the three present. As it turned out, our unit was decimated.

On the 21st of November, we were still in a cleanup operation in the vicinity of Suggerath, probing a little here and a little there trying to establish a stable line with our units to the north and south of us. Although our commanders supposedly knew what was going on in the overall scheme, the enlisted foot soldier knew little except the terrain he could view with his own eyes. I had no idea where Company K and Company I were located or what they were doing. Companies I, K and L were the three rifle companies of the Third Battalion, 333rd Regiment and Company M was our heavy weapons company. It was not until I read of the 9th Army operations years later that I learned Company K was attacking on our left flank and Company I was on the right flank.

The weather itself had become most ominous with the severe drop in temperature and the incessant rain. Ninth Army Operations described it as follows:

The weather continued to support the enemy. XXIX TAC on 21 November flew 131 sorties, dropping 19 tons of bombs. The abnormal rainfall saturated the ground troops. Continual enemy fire forced them below ground, but water flowed, or seeped, into their foxholes, and sometimes poured in over the tops of their overshoes. The men were taught to guard against trenchfoot, but care and dry socks were an impossibility in a sector where a man stood all day long to his knees in icy water, constantly on the alert for attack.

✻

The Third Battalion was on the attack on November 21, but the brunt of that attack was provided through Company I and Company K. Company L supposedly was assigned a new company commander as a replacement on November 21, and I never heard of the new commander. A description of what was going on is described in the Ninth Army Operations as follows:

The route of attack for the 333d Regiment lay to the northeast, generally along the railroad track joining Suggerath and Würm. The Würm River was to remain as the boundary line between companies.

(Terrain) The highway linking the two villages ran to the left of the railroad track. Farther to the left a small wooded area bordered the Würm River, but pillboxes at 895659 covered it and the thicket dwindled to nothing at the southern extremity to Müllendorf. The extreme left of the battalion zone consisted largely of open fields bounded by hedges and trees with small, scattered woods, but these, denuded of leaves, offered scant concealment. Photo interpretation revealed no pillboxes here. A large chateau, surrounded by small buildings at 889665, was suspected to be a possible enemy strong point.

Armored assault against the terrain northeast of Suggerath was difficult. On 20 November drizzling rain turned the loamy soil into a quagmire, and 21 November saw no change in the weather. Two tank approaches to the enemy positions were considered. One, the highway Suggerath-Würm, was thoroughly mined. The high ground to the right of the railroad track offered a possibility, but the only method of reaching this high ground from Suggerath without exposure, was through the underpass at 889655. The underpass was not wide enough to permit passage of a Sherman tank.

At 1400 Colonel Pedley [Col. Timothy Pedley, Regimental Commander, 333rd Battalion], ordered the battalion commander to move back into the town of Suggerath where he would be in less personal danger.

Speaking to Major Lanou, Colonel Barrett [Col. Tandy Barrett, Commander, 3rd Battalion] said:

"The pillboxes from the high ground are strafing the infantry and holding their movement to practically nothing."

Colonel Barrett then called the OP on his radio.

"Let me talk to Three. Hello Blanton [Captian Ed Blaton, Intelligence Officer, 3rd Battalion]! You and Burns run things. Keep talking to Mitchell [Company I Commander]. He's gotta move. Get another telephone line started to here and see if we can keep it in. You stay up there and fight this thing. They are sore back there because we haven't taken Würm yet." It was then 1415.

A few minutes later he called his S-3 again and reiterated his order to be passed on to Company I.

"Are you holding K back? Good. Company I hasn't advanced far enough yet."

Shortly after this conversation was finished the radio operator reported: "I Company wants the artillery lifted."

The colonel called Blanton again.

"Raise the artillery barrage 200 yards and tell Company I to get advancing" and to Burns: "You and Blanton keep this thing going, one on the radio and one on the telephone. We're bogged down with

88s firing point blank."

The radio operator again listened for messages and within a few minutes, said: "Company I wants the artillery and mortar stopped at once. He says it is hitting our own men. The 2d Platoon is right around the box and our mortars are falling there."

"How the hell do they know whose artillery it is with all that stuff falling out there?" was the colonel's remark.

At 1500 21 November Major Cline Lampkin, S-3 of the regiment, visited Colonel Barrett. He inquired if the colonel would like assistance with the telephone or radio.

"Hell no! I'd like to fight a war, only I'm in the wrong place instead of up front," was the reply.

At 1500, the battalion commander called his OP.

"Get word to Mitchell to go on and get out of that artillery. As long as he stays there he'll continue to get casualties. It's worse than if he went on."

The colonel had been unable to contact Company I either by radio or telephone. He had lost contact with Company K about an hour previously and this condition persisted for the remainder of the day.

At 1520 the radio operator got Captain Mitchell. The colonel took the radio immediately.

"Hello, Mitchell. Pal, I know you're catching it hard, but you've got to keep moving. Go by infiltration and move forward. Leave that platoon by the box and bypass it. I've committed Company L to help on your right. The back end is blowing its top back here, but I know how tough it is. The tank destroyers are trying to get up. Let's see if we can't get this thing moving."

Major Lampkin returned to the regimental CP in Geilenkirchen at 1533, with these instructions from Colonel Barrett:

"Tell Colonel Pedley that these men are fighting and dying up here. No one is lying down. But we gotta have power to do this thing."

On Wednesday, November 22, our platoon was assigned a new lieutenant to replace Lieutenant Red Guerry, and Lieutenant Richard W. Schupe from Company F, Second Battalion was assigned as the third Company Commander for Company L since November 19. It was on Wednesday, November 22, that we embarked on what was to be our final attack of the Siegfried Line. It was raining and muddy. Squeak Williams was first scout and I was second. As I recall, we started east at about 3:00 p.m., and the only orders which I received were to advance forward until pinned down. We were to have a rolling barrage of our own artillery ahead of us. We were attacking the Würm River Valley and headed toward Müllendorf and the City of Würm. We got caught in cross artillery fire at the mouth of one pillbox, which luckily was filled with German civilians. I was fortunate enough to jump in a shell hole and be spared. One of my buddies was in the shell hole with me and he was struck by a direct artillery blast, and the last I saw of him he was hobbling on a bloody stump to the pillbox. I have no idea who he was.

Squeak was in the hole ahead of me, and we were still charged with orders to advance until we were pinned down. Rolled barbed wire was ahead of us, but I cleared that obstacle with such ease that it was no obstacle. We kept charging and darting and I do not really remember all that happened. One reacts by instinct and training. We would pass by a dead German and just keep on going. We came to a big farmhouse and things eased for a while. It was there that I picked up a huge red apple and put it in my ammo bag. We had the Würm River on one side and tank traps on the other. Although we did not know it at the time, it was subsequently learned that we were being sucked into a trap. The gentle meadow had been a field of green in mid-afternoon; by the time we had crossed it, it had the appearance of plowed ground due to the artillery bursts.

We were still attacking in an easterly direction along the southern edge of the Würm River. We then moved into the edge of the next little farm community, which I would later learn was Müllendorf. At that time, I thought perhaps we were on the edge of Würm. I don't know how many of our officers had seen maps of this terrain, but I am sure that the field grade officers were thoroughly briefed and had a fair idea of the game plan. The information which trickled down to the platoon and squad level was negligible. All that we knew at our level was simply to move easterly toward Würm until pinned down.

As we moved into the edge of Müllendorf, we were confronted with a large farm complex consisting of brick, stone and masonry buildings all tied together in one huge operation. Squeak and I entered into a courtyard through two huge doors and a fairly complete farm community was housed in this setting. There were a series of residential units tied together on our right and stables, and the usual barns and outbuildings were contained in the complex. Squeak and I immediately started to secure the area. Through the entrance to the first living area we surprised two SS troopers. They surrendered without a struggle and were sent to the rear by one of our sergeants. There was a clash across the street, and we heard that Erickson was killed. We didn't know at the time who was killed and wounded. Dark was upon us, and we went through the outhouses and stables trying to secure the area. We learned that there were remnants of our company and parts of another battalion with us.

The replacements were recognizable as ours only by uniform. I was fortunate to be with some with whom I had trained. There was comfort in being known and being a part of a group which had trained as a unit. Surely, the plight of the replacement must have been unbearable, to be thrown into such an impossible life and death situation and yet be a complete stranger. There must have been some solace, however, since a replacement would not feel the pain of learning that a close buddy had just been killed or maimed.

Robert Rachofsky was our company radio man. He was with our new company commander, who had joined us just before the attack.

The enemy had a way of tracking our 300 radio with artillery, and Rachofsky warned us not to stay around him as the artillery had been getting next to him all afternoon. His 300 radio was our only communication to the rear. He and our new company commander, Richard W. Schupe, were just outside the huge barn where Squeak and I had captured the two Germans. A heavy wooden gate separated them from Squeak and me. Rachofsky cut the radio on to try to get communications with our rear, and the Germans zeroed in with an 88 and made a direct hit on them. This knocked out our radio communications and killed Rachofsky and our new company commander instantly.

Within the area were a part of our platoon, a part of our third platoon, and remnants from the second battalion. At this point, our own artillery, plus the enemy's, came in on us in such a deluge that we sought refuge in a series of cellars. We were then surrounded by the enemy, but were unaware of it. The 10th SS Panzer unit of the Germans had moved into the area, but this was not known to our intelligence. The panzers, with mounted 88s, surrounded the area and counter-attacked. A sergeant from the second battalion was able to converse in German and, after a time, our officers were forced to surrender those of us who were left.

While we were in these cellars, at least three of our artillery shells hit us directly. At that point, I reached in my ammo bag and retrieved the large red apple I had gotten from the farmyard that afternoon. I took a big bite, popping it as they do and whispered to Squeak, perhaps rather loudly, "Gee, just like a movie, ain't it?" I remember this distinctly because Squeak Williams heard this remark, and we have had occasion since then to relive some of this.

I have later learned that a part of the group captured with me were two men from Company K and a part of Company F of the Second Battalion. You can't imagine the chaos which is present in such a campaign as this, and in reading some of the operation accounts years later, you discover that chaos was prevalent in the rear also. Excerpts from the Ninth Army Operations are quoted here to give some idea what was going on around us at the time.

84th Division. During 21 and 22 November the 84th Division and the 405th Infantry Regiment of the 102d Division encountered elements of the German 15th Panzer Grenadier Division and the 10th S.S. Panzer Division, these having supplemented the 183d Volksgrenadier Division. The new formations defended their ground with far more vigor than the 183d displayed.

Müllendorf and Würm. The 309th Engineer Battalion attacked the underpass north of Suggerath on the morning of 22 November, blowing it apart with two charges. A bulldozer included in the plan failed to appear.

The 3d Battalion of the 333d Regiment was to
continue the attack. Division had released the 2d
Battalion to lend its aid on the left of the sector.

1st Lieutenant Joe Robinson, liaison officer of
the 325th Field Artillery Battalion, gave his British
colleague the fire plan overlay, which was to be
passed on to each tank commander, thus providing
the artillery with an abundance of observers.

"Where is the artillery going to place its initial
fires?" Colonel Barrett asked, when checking on the
readiness of the 3d Battalion to move out at 1100.

"My battalion is going to fire four volleys into
the valley and move it up," replied Robinson. "If
the tanks start at 1100 or 1102 it will be all right.
The entire corps artillery is going to fire on the
ridge north of Suggerath. I don't believe we'll have
trouble with the 88s today. We've plastered hell out
of them."

1st Lieutenant Schupe arrived to command
Company L and Colonel Barrett oriented him as
follows:

At the present time Company I is on the right
and K on the left of the Würm River. Company K
can advance and is ahead of I. We are holding Company K until I is able to advance. The 2d Battalion is
coming up on our left. Company L is in the draw at
897653. They didn't get off yesterday when I wanted
to commit them. We have a man to guide you up.
Lieutenant Ponticrevo is the best officer in the company. I know those men in the company want to go.
I'm going to use one platoon with Lieutenant
Ponticrevo to follow the tanks and mop up so the
engineers can blow these boxes. We jumped off yes-

terday and didn't get any farther than I can throw a rock, except on the left where it was fairly easy. If you get a chance to talk to the officers when you get out there, push them. Send Lieutenant Kronberger to Company I to help Captain Mitchell out.

The colonel then issued an order to check all forms of communication.

At 1055, Lieutenant Colonel Barrett attempted to get Company K without success.

"Give me I Company. Mitchell? Any of our artillery falling yet? No artillery yet! Well it should be soon. Smoke will be coming down now (1110). How close is it coming down? Think it will help? You can move it, you know."

"Here's the first mess up already," commented Colonel Barrett, following this conversation. "The tanks aren't out there yet."

The account of the attack was related by Captain Mitchell, commanding Company I:

We jumped off again at 1200 with a good artillery barrage. The 81mm's did a good job that day, too. I gave the 1st platoon to Staff Sergeant Patches, the 2d to Lieutenant McDonald, and the 3d platoon to Technical Sergeant Hubbard. I sent the 1st and 2d up again over the same routes and kept the 3d in support. One platoon of British tanks, with flame throwers mounted, was supposed to move out with us. One platoon of Company L was to follow the tanks, mop up and occupy the pillboxes as we went along.

The flame throwers couldn't get under the bridge because the engineers hadn't cleared it. We had to jump off without them. At this point Lieutenant McDonald showed a lot of leadership. Many of the men didn't want to attack without the support they had been promised. They knew it would be the same as the day before. McDonald got up, yelled to the men to follow him, and started out across the field alone. He was under fire from mortars and machine guns immediately. The entire company began to move forward. They crawled up to the pillboxes — every inch of the way. By this time the 1st Platoon was once again in the woods under fire. The 3d was still in support.

The flame throwers finally got up behind the hill out of Suggerath and came across the field. The infantry-tank team began working on the first two pillboxes. A few squirts from the flame throwers and the Germans poured out of the two boxes and the trenches adjoining them. The bastards are afraid of those flame throwers and won't be caught inside a box when they move up.

Initially 16 to 18 prisoners came out of the first two boxes, and later 20 came out of the third. We gave them a chance to surrender because we knew they would quit if given a chance and we didn't want to have to dig them out.

The 1st Platoon, still in the woods, had moved up abreast of the 2d Platoon on their right.

Once we were able to take the first pillboxes, the flame throwers went down to the next group of fortifications. The men were able to go down the connecting trenches and it was comparatively easy. After about three more boxes had been taken, the fuel trailers on the tanks bogged down and the men couldn't move them. They used demolition on the trailers and went on to help us clean out.

The 1st Platoon, keeping abreast, had knocked out a machine gun in its sector. The men moved forward when harassing fire from their flank was eliminated by reduction of the pillboxes.

I tried to get the tanks to come with me into Müllendorf but the tank commander said they had no orders to go any further and would not go.

We reorganized along the hill on which the pillboxes had been knocked out and started toward Müllendorf without the tanks.

When we took the boxes, my 3d Platoon pulled up even with the 2d Platoon on the left.

We reached a pillbox by the railroad tracks. The Germans had abandoned it just before our arrival, had it covered by fire, and every time we tried to occupy it we paid. One man was killed and two wounded trying. It was covered by snipers in the vicinity, and from fire to the north. We never could get into the damn thing.

Company F of the 2d Battalion, which had come up to our left and joined us, was there to help. Its company commander, Captain John F. Tye, volunteered to follow us into Müllendorf, keeping to the right of the railroad track.

When we had reached this pillbox by the railroad, Company F was abreast of us and we were all receiving accurate small arms and artillery fire from Müllendorf, keeping to the right of the railroad track.

We pulled back to a position in front of the pillboxes and began to get set for the night. I decided to move back, because the terrain to the rear was more adapted to defense than the ground on the outskirts of Müllendorf. It meant giving up 250 to 300 yards.

The 1st Platoon, under Sergeant Patches, had moved through the woods and gone into Müllendorf. I knew they were gone because I had given them our plan when we reorganized and told them what to do. I sent a small patrol into Müllendorf to see if they could get the platoon out, or locate it. They were unable to get into the town. The Germans sent up flares and had machine guns covering the outskirts. Sergeant Hartwell was killed on the patrol. The rest got back.

After two full days of striving against heavy odds in weather which kept the ground soft and soggy, and without adequate support, the 3d Battalion of the 333d Infantry was a battle-weary organization. Lieutenant Colonel Barrett was just as haggard and tired as any of his unit commanders. Regimental orders kept him in a CP in Suggerath.

In contrast to the first morning, when he had been clean shaven and ready to do battle, on the morning of the third day he was tired. He had hardly slept or eaten more than a biscuit since the attack crossed the line of departure the first morning. His voice was low and he walked slowly when he moved about in his basement CP.

The weather had come in on the side of the enemy, interfering not only with the progress of the assaulting troops, ground, and air, but seriously hampering supply and transportation.

Colonel Barrett recently mentioned to me that he felt we were going on a wild goose chase that afternoon and he held up the attack until he was forced to move. We obviously ran into more armor than had been anticipated. Those of us who survived have been trying to put the pieces together, and letters from a member of the Second Battalion give an idea of what we ran into. They were written to my Sergeant Cornelius Abraham, who was captured with me, and they are produced here.

2324 Kendall Avenue
Madison, Wisconsin 53705
August 3, 1965
Dear Mr. Abraham:

Your letter printed in the July 1 issue of the *Railsplitter* mentioned that you were captured on November 22, 1944 and the date plus the fact that you were in L Company of the 333rd suggest that this may have occurred during the attack on Müllendorf. If this is correct I thought that you might be able to answer some questions that have bothered me for some time.

I was in F Company of the 333rd and as you may remember, we were tangling with a few pillboxes on the hill right in front of Müllendorf that same day. Two of our platoons got separated from the company and I had heard that they had later joined up with elements of L Company and gone into Müllendorf where they were mostly captured or killed. I wonder if you know anything about this and if you remember any of these men. Right now, the only name that I can remember is that of Sergeant Lucania, but I would probably recognize others if I heard them. I would also be interested in anything that you might be able to tell me of the death of Lieutenant Schupe who was CO of F before he transferred to L.

LEST WE FORGET

One man from L Company ended up in the same pillbox that I was in for three days. His name was Sergeant Santoro and he was wounded either the first or second night that we were there.

I would appreciate any information you could give me on the above questions and in any case I would be interested in hearing what happened to you that day. Do you know anything about which Kraut units were in that area and how strong they were? Also wonder how the Krauts handled prisoners under battle conditions.

I hope that all of these questions are not too much of an imposition to you.

Sincerely,
Frank Freese

*

2324 Kendall Ave.
Madison, Wisconsin
September 21, 1965
Dear Mr. Abraham—

I would like to thank you for your interesting letter of August 13, 1965 and to apologize for the delay in this reply. I particularly appreciate your information as to the fate of Lieutenant Schupe. He was certainly a fine man; one who deserved much better than he received. You may be correct about the village of Würm (rather than Müllendorf as I suggested). Unless L Company was better informed than F, it was hard to tell where you were (or why) about 90 percent of the time.

You certainly had a rough time of it in the Siegfried Line and I'm glad that you were able to survive it all. Far too many were less fortunate. I was one of the very lucky ones who survived the whole business with no major injuries (but lots of misses). Around Geilenkirchen our company was reduced from normal strength to 33 men within 3 days after we were put on the line. Even with replacements coming in we were cut down to 30 or 35 men on three different occasions.

As you know, after spending about a month around Geilenkirchen, the division was shifted down to Belgium for a while. Later they came back to the Roen River area and participated in the fight from the Roen to the Rhine and from the Rhine to the Elbe. None of it was pleasant and the Bulge in particular was frostbitten and bloody misery. But none of it was as bad as what you saw when we were first put on the line.

I might mention that I lived in New Orleans for about 8 years (1952–1960) and went through Lafayette several times. I have many wonderful friends down that way and hope that one of these days I'll get back down there to see them and possibly meet you.

Sincerely,
Frank Freese

✿

2324 Kendall Ave.
Madison, Wisconsin 53705
July 8, 1967
Dear Bob:

I would like to thank you very much for your informative letter of June 30. The details you provided fit in with previous information that I had and, in addition, filled in a few more gaps.

About all that I knew right after the war was that a Lieutenant William Tway had led a platoon of

Company F in an attack on Müllendorf, supporting
a 3d Battalion force (Sergeant Joseph Gray was a
member of this platoon). The last that we heard of
them was a radio call from Lieutenant Schupe saying that he was entering (or in) Müllendorf with our
platoon. His message was cut off by what someone
claimed was a direct hit. According to our Battalion
records it was later learned that Müllendorf was occupied by 8 SS regiments, 2 Panzer regiments, and
an artillery unit. That's a fairly sizable crowd of
Germans for part of one American battalion—even
if they were Railsplitters.

Your account of what happened in Müllendorf
agreed remarkably well with what I had heard from
Mr. Cornelius Abraham (112 Wallace Drive,
Lafayette, Louisiana 70501), who was in L Co.,
333rd and was also captured on that day. Mr.
Abraham also thought that he was captured in
Würm. Could be that you are both correct. If so,
you must have passed through or around
Müllendorf since you started near Suggerath and
attacked up the valley at the Würm River (on our
left flank). After the attack we held some pillboxes
on a hill overlooking Müllendorf. There were some
men from 3d Battalion on our left and a few of
them mixed up with the remnants (less than 40
men) of our company. Down in Müllendorf there
were several Krauts including one who was awfully
handy with an 88. We saw no sign of the woman
with the patched posterior and therefore had no
way of knowing that Doc Hooker had been there
and got to the seat of the problem.

Again, thanks for all of the trouble you have
taken to satisfy my cracked curiosity about some-

thing that happened to some friends more than twenty years ago. Best of luck to you and Harry Hampton. I hope that you Dartmouth Indians will have a bang-up reunion.

Best regards,
Frank Freese

Dear Cornelius:

Thought that you might be interested in this letter. Bob Hooker (105 Edgewood R., Westwood, Mass. 02090) was a medic with L Co. and was apparently captured the same day that you were. Perhaps you knew him.

Harry Hampton (60 Chestnut Ave., Larchmont, N.Y. 10538) was a replacement lieutenant who got into L Company a few months after you left.

My family also was corresponding and trying to learn of our fate, and the Army wrote Howard Hyle's parents a bit about our mission on that November afternoon and this letter is reproduced here.

PD/je

WAR DEPARTMENT
In reply refer to: The Adjutant General's Office
Washington 25 D.C.
PC-G-201
Hyle, Howard H.
(17 Feb 45) c50188 33732583

24 February 1945
Mr. and Mrs. Howard R. Hyle
1 Dutton Avenue
Catonsville, Maryland
Dear Mr. and Mrs. Hyle:

I am writing to you concerning your son, Sergeant Howard H. Hyle, who has been reported a prisoner of war of the German government, as you were informed in my telegram of 21 February 1945.

A report regarding the circumstances under which your son was initially reported missing in action has now been received in this office in reply to an inquiry dispatched to the Commanding General of the European Theater of Operations. This report states that Sergeant Hyle was an assistant squad leader in a force which had been assigned the task of attacking the town of Müllendorf, Germany. The point of departure of his organization was Suggerath, Germany, and its ultimate destination was Würm, Germany. This force was last observed on 22 November 1944 entering Müllendorf, after which small arms fire was heard and contact with the group was lost. The report was subsequently received from the German government, through the international Red Cross, that your son has been taken prisoner during this operation.

The knowledge that your son is alive, although a prisoner of war, has, I feel, somewhat alleviated your anxiety.

Sincerely yours,
J. A. Ulio
Major General
The Adjutant General

Howard Hyle, Bill Long and I had become fast friends during the Camp Claiborne days, and we had furnished each of our families with addresses in order that they could communicate in the event some untoward event interrupted our communications. The families spent many hours comforting each other and seeking information about their sons.

Between the time we moved to the front on Friday, November 17, 1944, and the night of Wednesday, November 22, 1944, our platoon had been decimated to the point that only five of the original members remained. Everyone else was either killed, wounded or captured. Of those five remaining, I learned years later that three were killed and the other two wounded. Lieutenant Coakley's admonition at the monastery the week before that only one third of us would be done in was vastly underestimated. Our intelligence had badly underestimated the opposition and no one apparently knew of the Panzer Divisions which had moved into position.

It was hard to realize that for all of our training our battle was to cease after five days. No longer would we drop German blood on German soil, and our mission thereafter became one of survival in a different environment.

I had the satisfaction of having been a part of this great event, however. I had put myself on the line for my country, and I was pleased that I could do my own thing and not have someone do it for me. This was one of the things of which I had constantly reminded my mother during my period of training.

After having gotten into combat in what was some of the roughest fighting of the war, I soon realized that there was no way that I could go unscathed. The odds simply were not with those in the original unit. I knew that I could meet death at any moment, but I felt that I would just be wounded. It never entered my mind that I would wind up as a prisoner of war. I don't believe any soldier ever thinks of himself as being a prisoner at any time. *Death*—yes; *wounded*—yes; *prisoner*—no!

CHAPTER III

STALAG XIB

COMBAT HAD SUDDENLY come to an end for me, and it was hard to realize that I had become a prisoner of war. Little did I realize, however, that although combat was over, my real battle was just commencing.

We were ordered to drop arms, which we did. I still had a hunting knife strapped about one of my legs, and I elected to keep it for the time being. The Germans wanted our cigarettes and chocolate. Although I didn't smoke, I carried a couple of packs as spares for my buddies.

Even with my initial contact with those Germans at the moment of our capture, there was an uncanny feeling of communication. Each one had been trying to kill me and I had been trying to kill him. Each knew the other was at the precipice of death, and I sensed a feeling of mutual re-spect. Each was as concerned about living and dying as was I, and there was the sort of understanding that baffles a fi-nite mind. We were shuttled to the rear by other German soldiers. We knew that Würm was scheduled to be bombed by our own planes that night, and we were anxious to get out of the target area. The Germans almost double-timed us with our hands behind our heads and every so often they fired their machine gun along the side of the road for our benefit. It seemed that we ran most of the night, but they did stop for a spell and housed us in an old building. We were then put into some vehicles and carried into Krefeld the following morning.

Thursday, November 23, 1944, was Thanksgiving Day, and we had been promised a hot meal by our mess crew on Thanksgiving. Our last hot meal had been the brandy breakfast on Sunday, November 19. Since that time, we had snacked as time permitted on cold K-rations and candy. Sleep had been nonexistent except for a stolen cat-nap here and there. Each foxhole was paired with two men and one had to remain awake at all times for security purposes. The night of the twenty-second meant no sleep at all for the group.

We were unloaded from army trucks in downtown Krefeld shortly after daybreak. There we were displayed for the civilians to gaze upon, and then we were escorted into an army camp. At this point, they took our helmets and rain gear, and it was our understanding that this equipment was later used to disguise the Germans in the Battle of the Bulge. We were kept in several rooms in this army camp, and we were stripped and searched. I elected then to get rid of my hunting knife, because I did not know what the future held. We were searched and each of us gave our name, rank and serial number. The Germans knew our division and when we had left the States. As I recall, their interrogation occurred on the afternoon of November 23. I believe we were offered some form of food or soup that evening. It is my recollection, however, that I wasn't in the mood for food, particularly what they had to offer, and I declined.

One of the agonies of being a prisoner was thinking of home and what an ordeal it would be for my family. Before combat I felt that somehow I would be able to manage and survive. After receiving my baptism of fire, I realized that it would be miraculous to come out unscathed. After capture, I suppose I worried more about the plight of my family

than I did of my predicament. Little did I realize on
Thanksgiving Day that there would be a nine-month period
in which I would have no word from home, and all that I
could do would be just to think about them and worry
about them and pray for them. I frankly was more concerned for their welfare than my own, as I had an abiding
faith and was prepared to meet whatever destiny was mine.
I was in the frame of mind that I felt I could die with a
smile on my face.

I, of course, was not able to keep any of my mother's
letters, and one of her letters, written on Thursday, November 23, 1944, could not be delivered to me and was returned. It's ironic that the only letter that she wrote before
knowing of my capture was returned to her. It is also ironic
that the letter, written on Thanksgiving Day, was being
written just one day after my capture and about the same
time that the Germans were stripping us and searching us
in Krefeld. Her letter, which is copied here, will reveal
more about her and about the home in which I was reared
than anything I could tell you. If it had not been for my experience in Germany, we would not have this piece of her
handiwork. This to me is just one of the small ways in
which the Lord blesses and puts things in place.

No. 60
Thursday,
November 23, 1944
Dear Dan,

I'm thinking of you today wherever you are, and
trust you had opportunity to participate in some
service of Thanksgiving. I've been spending
Thanksgiving as usual going through regular routine
but listening to radio expound on our many reasons
for being thankful. I liked what "Mystery Chef" had

to say more than any other commentator, I believe. He is a living example of what faith and prayer can do for one. He said all of our great leaders were men of God. General Eisenhower, he said, had many books on military tactics but he carried only his Bible with him. He said General Marshall was a close and fervent man of prayer, and one who reads his Bible. Others he named were as good students of the Bible. He said he thought this was the greatest period in life to be alive, that he thought we were entering upon the greatest period in history, that things were developing as had been predicted in the Bible and if we would read, and read to understand and believe, we could see for ourselves. I know what he said is true.

Today, I am commending you to read your Bible each day, if it is at all possible. It will enrich your life and help you to understand things you never thought of before. It will help you to mount any obstacle, it will enlighten you, it will help you to bear your sorrows and disappointments, it will renew and increase your faith, it will cause you to be happier than you have ever been.

If I never did anything more than inspire you to live according to the principles of true discipleship, I would feel that I had done the greatest thing I could do for you.

I know you are always going to need the companionship of God now more than ever, so this Thanksgiving Day I felt a deep urge to talk about the more serious side of life—not that you are not endowed with all the traits of the most devout Christian—but I know from my own experiences, if we cast our burdens upon the Lord, He will carry us through the roughest places and I know God will carry you through and you are going to be one of His brightest stars. This Thanksgiving Day I'm thankful for you and Ray because I know that you are going to make the most of your opportunities and will be benefactors of mankind. So, I'm not grieving for you today but rejoicing that you are doing your part wherever you are and looking forward to that time when we shall be reunited.

Sue and I sat down and had Thanksgiving dinner together. Daddy and Mr. Mac went hunting. You know today was open for hunting. I hope they bring the quail home. They usually do when they go to Morton, where they went today. Won't it be great when you and Daddy and Ray can spend Thanksgiving hunting again. That may not be long.

We had planned to go home next weekend, make a visit and bring Highstepper home too. If Daddy gets off to the Army-Navy game as planned we will postpone our visit until the next weekend.

It is truly a wonderful, sunshiny, cool Thanksgiving here. I hope the sun is shining wherever you are. Did you get my letters regularly before you left England, and have you received any since arriving at your new destination?

I'll be seeing you tomorrow.

I love you,

Mother

Is it not strange that of all the letters she wrote to me before capture, this was the only letter that was returned to her?

On November 24, the Germans herded our group into some bare boxcars for what would ultimately become a four-day ordeal. Fortunately, we were in top physical condition at the time, and we were fortunate to be with some of the group with whom we had been captured. Two of our lieutenants were still with us, but our platoon leader had joined our unit only on November 21 or 22, and he was still pretty much a stranger to us. Nevertheless, it was consoling at that point to be with friends who had lived and trained together for some ten months.

Our captors provided three or four cans of inedible meat for the occupants of each boxcar. With forty-odd men to each car, this paltry ration was hardly enough to sniff at, much less to sustain you. Other than the occupants of each car and the few cans of meat, there was nothing else but the four bare walls. There was no hint of a latrine facility and no hint of even a drink of water. The fierce winter of 1944-45 had already made its appearance and the cold was almost unbearable. The cold caused frost to cover the interior of the bare walls, and we were able to lick the frost with our tongues to get some moisture into our systems.

There was not even the hay on the floor that we provide for shipment of cattle. The boxcars had no lights or windows except for two small windows in the upper corner of each car. These windows were not large enough for a man to escape and even so they were covered and crossed with barbed wire.

Our train of prisoners chugged back and forth across northern Germany for four days and nights. There was nothing for us to do inside but to sit or stand or lie in muted silence. I am sure none of us knew or could anticipate what our fate would be.

Much of the time our train simply remained on a siding for more important German shipments to be made. Of course, our Air Force was at work and the tracks would be bombed ahead of us or behind us, and it seemed that the journey would never end. Our forces couldn't tell our train from any other and we never knew when our train itself would be subject to bombing or strafing.

Fortunately, I had retained a German language handbook the Army had issued each of us, and I had had one semester of German language at Millsaps College. I, therefore, started to learn the language as best I could. I had still retained one package of cigarettes which the Germans had overlooked. As we were parked on a siding in some unknown German city on the second day of our journey, I was able to converse hesitantly with some German whom I took to be a civilian. He had an apple and I was able to trade my last package of cigarettes for his apple. He passed the apple to me through the small barbed window in the corner of the car. At that point, little did I know that American cigarettes were to become our medium of exchange.

We were not given a rest stop on that journey until dusk on the third day. The Germans stopped the train in a rural area and the guards unlatched our doors to let us go into an open field to relieve ourselves. Except for my bartered apple, there had been nothing to eat for the group except the few cans of meat given to each car.

On the fourth night of this trip, we pulled into a railroad station and ladies with the German Red Cross met us. They put a few bowls of porridge in the car with one spoon per bowl. We would pass a bowl from one to another. Each would take a few bites and the bowl and spoon would be passed to another. I still did not have much appetite but I did participate in a limited way. I recall that Squeak Williams ate with relish, however. I suppose we were all in sort of a stunned state, not yet realizing the plight in which we found ourselves.

On the fourth day of this train ride, we arrived at Stalag

XIB just outside of Fallingbostel. The winter had arrived full blast and the weather was miserably cold. We had already been weakened so much from the train ride and the elements that escape was unthinkable. The weather was ominous and if we had escaped into it, we surely would have frozen.

Stalag XIB must have housed thousands of prisoners. I suppose they had imprisoned men from many lands but for the most part we saw only troops captured on Germany's western front. Each nationality was housed in separate barracks and these barracks each housed some eight hundred men. Each was encircled with a high barbed wire fence with elevated guard houses located on each corner.

The barracks itself was unheated and of rough wooden construction. The interior consisted of one large open room with wooden bunks lined up in rows and four tiers high. The bunks were of rough lumber with slats to lie on. There was no mattress or hay of any kind for a bed. The interior was so well ventilated that frost even formed on the interior walls.

Prisoners were constantly being received and shipped from Stalag XIB, and some of the old hands kind of showed us the ropes after our arrival. The barracks to which we were assigned was essentially British, and I was able to commingle with some of the elite men of England, Canada and Australia who had parachuted into Arnhem, Holland, during September 1944. It was thought that if their mission could penetrate the German lines and secure a certain bridge that the Allies could encircle the Germans from the north and avoid having to attack the Germans broadside along the Siegfried Line. If the Arnhem attack had succeeded, it was felt the war would have been over by Christmas, 1944.

Such was not the case, however, and I was thrown in

with some of these gallant men who had been prisoners since September. When I first walked into my assigned barracks, one of these British soldiers had brewed a cup of English tea in a discarded can which he had fashioned into a serviceable cup. He offered to share a sip of his tea out of the tin can, and I must say that to this day I have never tasted such a delightful taste of tea as this. Of course, this was the first thing that I had had to drink since leaving Krefeld on November 24.

As we wandered into the barracks, we were told to locate an empty bunk that would be our domain. Fortunately, I was able to locate a ground floor bunk in the middle of the room near Bill Long.

Each person was issued half of a blanket and a metal bowl to receive the daily soup ration. There was a garbage dump at one end of the fenced enclosure and we soon learned to forage this dump to retrieve a usable tin can for culinary purposes.

Water and sanitary conditions were at a premium at Stalag XIB. There were a limited number of inside water faucets to serve each compound, and the Germans would leave the water on only for limited periods during the day. It was not unusual to stand in line an hour or more for a drink of water, only to have the Germans cut off the main valve just before you could partake of the long-awaited drink.

We were locked inside the barracks before dark each evening and there were no inside lights or latrines. Each prisoner would retire in his own little bunk and try to sleep among the restless bickerings and comments which permeated the night. You slept with all of your clothes on and if you dared take your boots off, you would use the boots as a pillow. You dared not let your boots out of sight as some men had been deprived of shoes and equipment, and looting was a problem. Fortunately, I was only relieved of my helmet and raincoat, and I managed to hold onto all of the clothing which I had worn into combat.

We were awakened each morning before sunrise and we were herded outside into subfreezing temperature for a countdown to see if anyone had escaped. Buckets of ersatz coffee were then brought to the barracks and each of us got a ration of this hot liquid. This brew was not really potable, but we learned that this might be our only source of drink for the day. Also, the coffee had been boiled and to that extent it was less dangerous than the questionable water supply. As best as we could determine, this coffee was some kind of parched grain.

After the daylight coffee break, we were locked out of the barracks until about 10:00 A.M. each morning. The weather was absolutely unbearable and we had no alternative but to walk a brisk pace counterclockwise within the fenced enclosure trying to keep warm. The ground was frozen and the temperature never appeared to rise above freezing during my entire tenure at XIB.

About mid-morning each day, we were given our first edible rations for the day. At daylight, we received the ersatz coffee, but there was no food. A loaf of black bread was doled out to each five prisoners at 10:00 A.M., and it was necessary for each group of five to divide the bread equitably. We obtained some sort of makeshift knife which was passed between each group to divide the bread. The cutting of the bread into five equal shares became a ritual, and the one using the knife was hovered over menacingly by the remaining four to be sure that the division was even. Of course, the bread itself was uneven and much discussion went into the measurements before the actual cutting proceeded. The crust was initially indented and after a consensus was reached on that, the bread was actually severed. To ensure equity, it was always agreed that the one doing the actual slicing would have the last piece after the other four had already chosen theirs. Fortunately, I had put three handkerchiefs in my pocket for combat and I used one handkerchief to wrap my bread. I would even slice my bread on the handkerchief so as not to lose any crumbs. Not one crumb was ever wasted.

It was necessary that each of us discipline himself so that the bread could be stretched out over the entire day. The bread itself was a sort of sourdough black bread which apparently was a staple of the German diet during those hard times. The bread purportedly had some sawdust in it, and straw from the grain was placed in the pans apparently to keep the dough from sticking to the pan. At first, the bread was considered inedible, but we soon learned that it would become one of our main sources of sustenance.

At morning ration time, we were also given a single pat of ersatz oleo or fat of some kind. In addition to this, each man was doled out one teaspoon of coarse sugar. We salvaged some small tin cans from the garbage heap to hold the butter and sugar.

During this morning ration period, I would slice one thin piece of bread from my portion and I would spread my fat on the bread. The sugar was then sprinkled over the fat, and this constituted my mid-morning breakfast.

It was not feasible to retain the sugar or fat as the little tin cans were not convenient to carry on your person. Each grain of sugar was meticulously salvaged and eaten. We would moisten our fingers and nails to retrieve each little grain from the crevice of the can. The remaining portion of the bread I carefully wrapped in the handkerchief and placed in my jacket pocket for safekeeping.

After the morning ration, we would continue our brisk walks trying to keep the body warm in the numbing cold. We had no hat or head cover, and our faces and ears would just about freeze. It was also during this time that we would stand in line to try to get a drink of water.

Each man had been furnished a metal soup bowl for our daily ration of soup. A central kitchen cooked the soup for the entire Stalag. A soup detail from each barracks was dispatched to the central kitchen at noon each day to pick up the soup. The soup was a watery conglomeration consisting either of some member of the cabbage family or some peas which had deteriorated so much they were almost inedible. Also, at the time our soup was distributed to us, we were given a small boiled potato. The potato also was frequently covered with rotten spots, and it usually was little larger than a golf ball. We soon learned that everything that was dispensed to us in the way of food was to be jealously guarded and eaten no matter how inedible we thought it to be.

You were indeed one of the lucky ones if you were selected to fetch the noon soup at the central kitchen as you were usually able to steal a few of the marble-sized potatoes to put in your pocket. Now, all was fair; whatever you could steal by hook or crook was yours. You had to do everything in your power just to survive.

A few days after our arrival at Stalag XIB, another trainload of prisoners arrived from the western front. I specifically remember that three members of the second platoon of Company L were a part of this group. Jerome Goodkin of Beverly Hills, California, Sergeant Martin Riley of Birmingham and Roger Melgary of White Plains, New York, were a part of this shipment. They stated they had been captured attacking a pillbox on Thanksgiving Day. Goodkin had been shot through one of his feet and he was trying to hop around with a stick. His wound simply had some tissue paper wrapped around it. The Germans apparently were just strapped for supplies and some of the wounded received little or no treatment.

Sick calls were allowed during the morning hours only, but little was done in the way of treatment. Everyone developed dysentery and diarrhea as a result of the horrible filth in which we lived and as a result of our debilitated conditions. It got to the point that sick call was really meaningless, but we would nevertheless take turns to go simply to get out of the environment of our barracks.

Sanitation conditions were beyond comprehension. The latrines were located outside of our barracks, and they did not even have running water. Putting it simply, the latrine consisted of nothing more than narrow slit trenches carrying a slight flow of water to carry away the waste. We had to stand or squat over this trench of water to rid ourselves of human waste. The trenches would dam up, and the entire latrine would become a big puddle of human excrement. Toilet tissue was a luxury only dreamed about. One has to be deprived of all creature comforts to realize how richly blessed we really are. Not only was there no tissue paper but also there was no paper of any description. We are used to so much and take so much for granted that one would have never thought that just a piece of paper could have meant so much.

At night, we were locked in our barracks, eight hundred men, sick with diarrhea and without water to drink, much less water with which to cleanse ourselves. If you had the urge of nature, which we all had in that condition, you would have to rap on the door and a guard would give you permission to walk to the latrine. There were no lights because everything was blacked out because of air raids. Once you got to the latrine at night, you would have to carefully enter as there was no way to discover whether it was dammed up and swimming with human excrement or not. In fact, even during daylight hours when it was dammed up, there was no way to safely step inside. It baffles the mind to discover just how much punishment the human body can withstand. It seems like a miracle that we could survive these conditions on such meager rations for such a prolonged period of time. And, of course, it wasn't a miracle but the handiwork of the One Upstairs.

Nearly every soldier who went into combat carried a pocket Testament with him. These had been furnished by the Army and there was a version for Protestant, Catholic and Jew. The Germans fortunately allowed us to keep our Testaments, and we spent much time in silent prayer and meditation and reading the scripture. We were sustained through His word.

After we had been in Stalag XIB for a few days, a Red Cross parcel was given to each four men. It was intended that each prisoner would receive one Red Cross parcel per week, and rations were provided in these parcels for a week's sustenance for one man. Each country prepared Red Cross parcels for its own, and the parcel we received at Stalag XIB was British-oriented. The American Red Cross box which we would ultimately receive was filled with ready-to-eat tins of meat and cheese. There was nothing to be prepared in the American parcel except for the instant coffee, unless, due to your own ingenuity, you tried to concoct something unusual out of the contents.

The British parcel which we received in early December, however, contained a large amount of unprepared food which had to be cooked. The British parcel contained powdered eggs, hot cereals, and the like, and it was necessary for us to cook each item together to share the end result with the four owners of the parcel. Our particular encampment had arranged to cook the ingredients over little individual fires on an open embankment in front of our barracks and just downhill from the latrine. The Red Cross parcel was the source of our evening meal. In northern Germany, the days grew very short and we had to be locked in the barracks by dark. Therefore, in mid-afternoon, the entire encampment would cover this barren hillside attempting to get a small fire started for the cooking process. Our metal soup bowl was our only cooking utensil, except for tin cans retrieved from the garbage dump. Fuel was scarce and we actually swiped boards out of our bunks to fuel some of the fires. This practice, of course, was forbidden by the Germans, and we would have to break up one board at a time and smuggle it outside to make the fire.

It was quite a sight to see these little groups of four men scattered over a frozen hillside attempting to kindle a little fire to cook a woefully inadequate portion. Bill Long and I shared the first parcel with two other prisoners. I cannot even remember who the other two men were. Nevertheless, the first attempt at cooking for the four of us was assigned to me. We all participated in building the fire and making the overall arrangements. Our first meal consisted of the dried eggs, which, when mixed with water and heated, would approach something resembling scrambled eggs. I managed to get these powdered eggs cooked in a fashion and then we had to go through the same ritual of dividing the eggs equitably just as we did the bread during the morning. This little ritual of exacting each portion proportionately was not a product of greed or selfishness. It just happened that it was a matter of survival and we wanted to see that each had an equal opportunity to survive.

As I have stated, I probably was more concerned about the welfare of my parents than I was my own. I feel that I was just consumed by the agony of not knowing how my parents would react to the news that I was missing in action. It would not be until February 1945 that they would actually learn that I was a prisoner and not dead.

On November 30, 1944, we were given our first opportunity to send a notification to our family. A copy of this limited notice is duplicated below.

Prisoner of War Camp

Date *Nov. 30 1944*.

(No. of Camp only; as may be directed by the Commandant of the Camp.)

I have been taken prisoner of war in Germany. I am in good health — slightly wounded (cancel accordingly).

We will be transported from here to another Camp within the next few days. Please don't write until I give new address.

Kindest regards

Christian Name and Surname: *DAN M. McCULLEN*

Rank: *PRIVATE FST CLASS*

Detachment: *AMERICAN INFANTRY*

(No further details. — Clear legible writing.)

Although this was written on November 30, 1944, my parents did not receive it until after February 23, 1945.

My parents probably suspected something was amiss when there was an interruption of mail, however. Around December 8 or 9, they received a telephone call from Bill Long's parents in Quincy, Illinois. Bill's parents advised Mother and Daddy that Bill was missing in action. They thus knew what they had already suspected, which was that we were in the middle of the Battle of Germany. Mother and Daddy therefore sensed that all was not well, as they knew Bill and I were in the same unit, and if he was in trouble, then I very likely would be in the same mess.

Therefore, when they received the knock on their door on the evening of December 10, 1944, they had the uneasy feeling that this was their notice of my predicament. At that time, the government telegram to my family was hand delivered by volunteers in order that some help might be offered to the family. Mary Lane Womack delivered this message of gloom to Mother and Daddy on the night of December 10, 1944. It was a strange coincidence that we lived around the corner from the Womack family when we first moved to Jackson in 1938. Mary Lane happened to be the sister of Dr. Noel Womack, who helped rear and treat each of my daughters through his pediatric clinic.

The message which Mary Lane delivered that night was simply a telegram advising Mother and Daddy that I was missing in action. A copy of that message appears below.

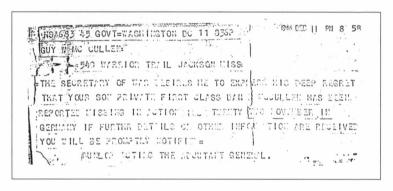

The Army then sent a formal notice on December 15, 1944, which is attached.

Mother and Daddy were blessed with a host of friends and an abiding faith, and the combination of the two sustained them in their hour of need. I still treasure a large box of letters of condolences received by Mother and Daddy from their friends all over this state and nation.

Although I had dispatched a restricted notification of my plight by the notice written on November 30, I was not able to write a message until December 9, 1944. For some reason, on that date, the Germans allowed us to write two cards from Stalag XIB. These were postcard type messages and the messages had to be very brief and noncontroversial, as they were censored by the Germans. Both of these cards are copied as follows:

December 9, 1944
Dear Mother,
    I have two cards this week. I'm making out O.K. Also, I'm assured of a safer and speedier return home so don't worry. I am just living for the return home. We will really have fun. Happy Birthday to you Sue.
    Love,
    Dan Buck

                         ✲

December 9, 1944
Dearest Mother,
    I hope you have seen my letter by now. I am still in a temporary camp. Most of my cooking is done by myself. I am doing O.K. though. I have received one Red Cross parcel. It really hit the spot. Please don't worry.
    Love,
    Dan

Space itself limited the message and we could not antagonize the Germans by saying anything derogatory. Also, we wanted to let the family know that we were reasonably safe without adding to their grief and uneasiness. Although these cards were written on December 9, 1944, Mother and Daddy did not receive one until February 1945, and they therefore suffered through the winter without knowing whether I was dead or alive.
    About the time that I wrote those cards on December 9, 1944, some of the fellows with whom I had been cap-

tured were shipped to other Stalags. Bill Long was separated from me about this time, and it was an added burden, being separated from such a good friend. It was not until the war was over that I learned he had been shipped to a northern naval station for interrogation. When he learned that he would be shipped out one morning, we were still sharing the first Red Cross parcel, and we then divided the parcel such that Bill could take some provisions with him, not knowing what kind of journey lay ahead of him.

Although Bill and I would not meet again until after the war, our families maintained a constant communication for the remainder of that winter and the ensuing years.

Life continued at Stalag XIB in much the same routine as we knew it before Bill's departure. The bitter cold continued to devastate us and, of course, our bodies were becoming more debilitated and emaciated. Our systems were losing their resistance to disease and infirmity. With lack of any bathing facilities, personal hygiene was something just dreamed about. Lice and probably other kinds of body pests infested our clothing. More and more men were falling out each day for sick call, but nothing was really accomplished by going to sick call.

I was fortunate in having worn such abundant clothing into combat, and I was even more fortunate not having been stripped of my clothing by the Germans.

I had worn an undershirt and shorts over which I wore a two-piece suit of olive drab wool long handles. I also had on my olive drab (OD) pants and OD shirt, both of which were of heavy wool. Over this, I had worn a GI issue OD wool sweater and this was topped with my combat jacket. I also had worn two pair of wool socks in my combat boots. The socks didn't last too long, but the other garments were still being worn when I was liberated months later.

One would think that with this much clothing we could

have withstood any kind of weather. With our bodies as weak as they were and with that winter being one of the worst winters in decades in northern Europe, it just seemed that we would ultimately freeze to death.

We dared not remove our clothing even for sleep as it would have been stolen. However, it was necessary to wear our clothing just to try to keep warm.

The German bread was so unpalatable that we utilized any means to try and dress it up. I well recall on one occasion that I thought I would try to make a part of my daily ration into a bread pudding. I added the pat of ersatz butter and sugar to it in my soup bowl and I retrieved two other ingredients from the Red Cross parcel. I believe there might have been a box of raisins of which a part was added. I then laboriously cooked the conglomeration over a fire on that barren hillside one afternoon. Once I had finished with the chore, I immediately set in to devour it. It had to be eaten with a spoon, and at the moment it was one of life's delicacies. I must say that it constituted a vast improvement over eating the dry, sour bread by itself. Little did I realize, however, that such a concoction was too rich for my run-down condition and it made me deathly ill. I thought that my stomach and bowel would never cease reacting to it. But it may have been that it was nothing more than coincidence, since everyone appeared to have similar symptoms.

We had no idea what our fate would be or how long we would remain at Stalag XIB. During the third week, however, we were marched in groups to a central bath house. This was a communal bath in the true sense. There was one large building with two large rooms divided by a solid wall. We were not aware of the exterminating chambers that later came to light at Dachau and other concentration camps, but this communal bath house could easily have served the same purpose at Stalag XIB. We were marched into one large room in which there were large overhead hooks. We were told to disrobe and hang all of our clothing on one of the hooks. We were getting our first bath since leaving Gerleen, Holland, in mid-November. When we were completely disrobed, we were ordered into the next room, which was equipped with an array of overhead showers. We were furnished a piece of very harsh soap, and the showers were then turned on by a master control. The water was turned on long enough for us to get wet all over and we vigorously lathered our bodies. The water was then cut off and we continued to lather and wash hoping to rid ourselves of body lice and other pests. After this proceeded for a time, the water was turned back on for rinsing purposes.

While we were in the shower room, our clothing hooks had been elevated by some master control and some kind of chemical or fumigating agent was burned in the sealed room to attempt to kill all of the lice and pests which hovered there. I must state that that bath and delousing attempt was a welcome respite from our usual routine at Stalag XIB. It had to boost our morale. This bath was one of the more meaningful baths that I took during those days. As I recall, I believe that I had two more baths before liberation was to come in May 1945.

Attempting to get some sleep in one of those large barracks was something else again. With that many men in a room there was constant bickering and disturbance. Army barracks in the States had been adorned with pinup pictures of movie stars and the like, and troops' conversations on Stateside centered on the pinups. Not so in prison camp. I don't remember a prisoner going to bed talking about anything but family and food.

We were all short-tempered, depressed and frustrated, and the nightly talk seemed to dwell on what we were missing and what we were looking forward to. I remember one boy described the chocolate party that he was going to have when he got home. He was going to have chocolate candy, chocolate cake and chocolate ice cream. He was going to have tables heavily laden with an assortment of these goodies and he would go into detail on how it would be arranged and served. This sort of chatter would just about drive some of the men nuts, but eventually everyone would drift into some sort of makeshift sleep. With that many men in one room, however, there was never a quiet moment as there was always some bickering and snoring and cavorting around.

CHAPTER IV

STALAG IIA

PRESUMABLY, the communal bath which we had enjoyed was to give us a good washing down in preparation for a mass move to another Stalag. On December 16, 1944, a large group of the prisoners at Stalag XIB was herded into barren boxcars for a grueling trip to the east. We were not furnished any news of the war and we had no idea how things were proceeding on the western front. I did not learn of the Battle of the Bulge until after liberation. It so happened, however, that the day we departed from Stalag XIB was also the beginning of the Battle of the Bulge.

We apparently were relatively safe from air attack by the Allies while in a Stalag, as our forces had learned of the locations of the large encampments. Once you left the Stalag, however, you were as subject to bombing or strafing as the enemy. Our freight train would look just like any other munition movement in Germany, and as we chugged back and forth across northern Germany, the tracks were bombed and the movement came to a standstill. Also, our train was frequently parked on a siding to let the more important German shipments proceed.

Little did we realize that when we were herded into these barren boxcars on December 16 we would not depart from them for four days and nights. We still had partial Red Cross parcels, and this was our only source of food for the next four days. As usual, we were housed in boxcars with approximately fifty prisoners herded into each car. Unlike the previous four-day trip to Stalag XIB, however, the Germans had covered the wooden floor with straw. I cannot remember whether I was allowed to take my one half blanket from Stalag XIB or not. The car I was in had the same type of one-by-three-foot window in the upper corner of the car. This was the only source of light and, of course, this was not adequate to see even what you were trying to eat out of your parcel, much less for reading of your New Testament.

Our physical condition was much worse during this trip than at the time of our first ride from Krefeld to Stalag XIB. All of us were in an emaciated state, suffering with diarrhea and dysentery. Some of the men were still suffering from open wounds received in battle. The wounded had received little medication, and gauze was unheard of. What first aid treatment was rendered consisted of some bandages fashioned out of paper very similar to crepe paper.

There were so many prisoners in each boxcar that if we all sat, there would have been no room. If we all stood, there was room but it was impossible to maintain this posture for the duration of the trip.

We first had to make a neat pile of our Red Cross parcels in the center of the car. There were no latrine facilities in the boxcar and we had to fashion a latrine of our own. We heaped a pile of straw near one corner of one of the sliding doors, and this served as the latrine for the fifty occupants for the next four days. Our food storage necessarily was next to this primitive latrine facility.

I have not been able nor have I attempted to relate this trip to anyone during the last forty-odd years except to my wife. It was difficult to talk about it rationally, and I feel that the One Upstairs may have numbed our senses so we could cope with the situation. I once heard it said that He will not inflict anything on you without first giving you the strength to endure it.

Little did we know what the next four days held in store. We eventually arrived at Neubrandenburg, which was almost to the Polish border. We would travel one direction and then the other. Of course, army supplies and munitions had precedence. We were shuttled onto side tracks where we would wait hours on end. Our forces did not know which train carried munitions and which carried prisoners. There were strafings and bombings, and all of this time we were housed within this crowded car without heat, light or water. We were able to open some of our Red Cross provisions, but for four days and nights, there was not one drop of water to drink. The food problem, together with the lack of latrine facilities, the types of maladies suffered and the absence of water, compounded the problems. The cold was unbearable, but it probably did serve one purpose, which was to suppress the stench of our primitive latrine to some extent.

We had no toilet tissue, but the absence of water to drink, much less to use for washing, made the tissue issue laughable.

Needless to say, we became so debilitated and weak, we literally wallowed in our own waste just as animals in transit do.

In spite of this, there was a spirit of cooperation among us. There had to be. When we slept, it was necessary that we place our heads to the outside walls and plant our feet to the center. It was also necessary that we lie on one side, since there was no room to lie on our backs. By lying on one side much like dominoes, with our heads to the outside, we could stack our feet on top of each other and at least assume a reclining position for an attempted sleep. When we got too tired of lying on that side, then all of the men in the car in unison would turn to the other side. This illustrates the degree of cooperation which we shared.

I suppose we kept warm in a fashion with our own body heat. Fortunately, it was so cold that the interior of the car frosted, and this was a source of moisture. Now, it is a little difficult to reflect on the time when these fifty-odd men were engaged in licking frost from the walls of that car without any regard to germs, sanitation, or the like.

I am not sure that I realized then what memories of the past and dreams of the future meant, and perhaps I did not realize what part faith plays in such a situation. I believe that it was probably then that I recognized that the only thing that separated us from swine or other animals was our faith. We were being carted about as if we were pigs en route to market, and we were like the pig except for our faith. Through this ordeal, however, there was a spirit of cooperation, and I do not recall any complaining. All of us were in one boat, and the name of the game was survival.

On the morning of the fourth day, we arrived at Stalag IIA on the outskirts of Neubrandenburg. Needless to say, some of our men were carried off these cars feet first. Where I got off was a rural road which had been trampled back and forth by the work animals pulling wagons. The hoof marks of these animals had trapped moisture before the freeze, and we were able to break chunks of ice out of these hoof marks to give us needed water. We did not know how much of this ice consisted of ingredients other than water, but it served the purpose at the time and we gladly partook of it. To reflect back on that four-day trip now, it is difficult to understand how we were able to survive it. It does point out the amount of punishment our bodies can absorb and what a wonderful creature we happen to be. We truly have to be the handiwork of the Master Craftsman, and through our faith and prayers, He saw us through this ordeal.

We departed from that train frozen, thirsting, and hurting. As mentioned, some were carried off feet first. I gladly ate the ice from the hoof prints, not caring or worrying about the impurities it contained.

We were then hustled into a large encampment containing prisoners from all over Europe. We were housed in large wooden barracks, not unlike those at Stalag XIB. Nationalities were housed together. Some of the streets were separated by barbed wire and the whole encampment was completely secured by guards, wire and bars. The daily routine was much as we had experienced at Stalag XIB. The latrine facilities were antiquated, but still much superior to Stalag XIB in that they were elevated over a pool of water and you did not have to wade in.

Stalag IIA held Russians, Greeks, Italians, Dutch, French and Serbians. In fact, every nation of Europe was represented. Each group tried to retain its lifestyle and heritage. The Italians received Red Cross parcels which included ingredients to make spaghetti. They rubbed the dough between the palms of their hands to make each stick of spaghetti.

I recall receiving one Red Cross parcel at Stalag II around Christmas. This was a whole parcel to myself. It had a pipe and a can of tobacco in it. I had never smoked but I lit a pipe of this tobacco. It burned my tongue and did nothing else for me, so I gave it away. I later learned that the tobacco was a medium of exchange which would help me survive.

The Russians were really hard-pressed because their country did not belong to the Geneva Convention, which permitted the Red Cross parcels. They had nothing to survive on except what the Germans provided.

Christmas Eve was a very special occasion in that the Germans let the barriers down among different nationalities. The Russians enjoy life and love music. A group of Russians came into our compound with violins and played some of their music for us. Happiness is a relative thing, and it was a very happy occasion. There was a joviality not previously experienced by us.

Even Christmas dinner was something special because it was sauerkraut. Our soup normally was cabbage soup with a few cabbage leaves floating around, and the sauerkraut furnished us something to chew.

Work details were assigned at Stalag IIA. Some had to go to the woods and cut wood to heat our compound. Some worked in a candy factory from which they smuggled sugar in their filthy clothing. This was accomplished by slitting a pant's pocket, tying a cord around your pant's leg, and letting the sugar settle around your ankle.

On one day, I was assigned to a brewery. Our job was to cut ice from a pond to store for the summer beer market. The Germans are famous for their beer. Before we started working that morning, we were each given a bottle of beer. In the winter, the Germans immerse the bottles of beer for a few minutes in a hot bucket of water. It may have been that this was to free the cap so that it could be opened. The bottles were not disposable and the cap was attached with a metal wire.

We cut ice all day in subfreezing weather without any food. The ice must have been about a foot thick, and we would chip it off in manageable chunks, run it up a chain ladder, and store it in an underground pit. Some experience for a Mississippi farm boy! And the weather was so frigid I cannot describe it.

It was at Stalag IIA that we were photographed and given our prison number. My prison number was 160422 and it was cut into a metal dog tag for identification should anything happen to me.

I have no idea how many people or nationalities were housed together at Stalag IIA. All facilities were primitive but there was electricity. A burial detail worked each morning, removing those who had expired the day and night before. A horse-drawn wagon waddled aimlessly through the dirt streets removing the bodies of those who would never more walk upon this earth. One is reminded of Gray's thoughts as he penned his "Elegy" and wondered what "gem of purest ray serene" was there buried on an ocean floor or what desert flower bloomed unseen except for One.

At Stalag IIA, a few books were available for reading pleasure. It is difficult now to reflect back on the conditions we then experienced. Needless to say, I was not in a frame of mind to read. I can remember attempting to read a book, only to cast it aside—we had been so dehumanized that we weren't capable of reading. I suppose during that first five or six weeks we were so deprived of sustenance and elements of life that we just clung to life and hope. Even if we could have escaped, we probably would not have because there would have been no chance of survival. The weather was unbearable. Our bodies were so under-nourished we were just barely holding on. There was a language barrier, and there was no place we could have gone except to the open country. Except for the presence of God, we could not have made it.

CHAPTER V

GÜSTROW

ON JANUARY 4, 1945, about twenty of us were moved
from Neubrandenburg to Güstrow. Güstrow was west of
Neubrandenburg and a few miles south of Wismar and
Rostock. We were housed in prefab barracks on the edge of
the city dump and were to work on various and sundry
jobs. Our principal work was for a construction company.
Our barracks was situated within a barbed wire enclosure.
Our guards had their own quarters at an opposite end of
the building. Our twenty men occupied one large room
where wooden bunks surrounded a pot-bellied stove. There
were no toilet facilities except for a water faucet in a room
connecting our sleeping quarters with another large room
which was to house an additional forty Americans. A makeshift kitchen was housed in a building in one corner of the
prison yard. One of our men in the first twenty was selected as our cook. He had been shot in the thigh during
capture and was unable to work. He was also no cook, but
that did not matter, since there was nothing to cook. Whatever the Germans gave us was thrown in the pot for so-
called soup.

On the first day of our arrival, soup was already prepared and delivered to us in the evening.

It was in a large tub and enough for sixty men. Our
other contingent of forty men did not arrive for several
days. The original twenty ate this soup with relish for three

days. Our systems were such that we could not eat as much as we imagined we could. On the third day, the soup spoiled, and we could not eat any more of it. Not wanting to let the Germans know that they had overfed us, we tore a hole in our floor and poured the spoiled soup in the hole. The tub was licked clean, and for all the Germans knew, we had eaten the whole thing.

Our complement was built up to sixty men around mid-January. An outside johnny was built for use during the day only. A trough was built leading to a gaping hole in the ground for a urinal. A can was placed inside the barracks for the sixty of us to use at night. There were no bathing facilities whatsoever.

The bunks were wooden and double-decked. We had a straw mattress and a flannel blanket of sorts. I chose a lower deck bunk next to a window, thinking the air might be a little more palatable near the window, and I would also have enough light to read when time permitted.

Until the bombings started in April, we worked from sunup to sunset, Monday through Friday, and until noon on Saturday.

Initially, the workdays were not too long because we were so far north there was not much daylight. The guards would wake us up about one hour before work time. We would toast a piece of German black bread on the top of the stove for breakfast. Red Cross parcels were intended for one week's sustenance, but we never received a parcel per week. At Güstrow, we probably averaged one parcel every three weeks. We at least were given our own parcel, and it was up to each of us to discipline our use of the contents. They usually contained five packs of cigarettes, spam, cheese, instant coffee, cream, vitamin pills and similar snacks. A D-bar was an enriched chocolate bar used as a cold ration for troops in combat. Most parcels contained one D-bar. It was not particularly good chocolate, but I could not discipline myself to eat one little section at a time. I would, therefore, make one meal out of it once it was opened. I would lie on my bunk and bite one small parcel at a time and just let it melt and run down my throat.

The savoriness of one of those occasions is one of my pleasant memories of that winter. The D-bar was rather coarse and crumbly. It was designed to give you certain food values, vitamins, and minerals, and was never intended to be a gourmet's delight. I can still remember fondly those moments when I lay on my bunk rolling a piece of that chocolate around on my tongue until it melted and coated all of my taste buds. It was one of life's most pleasant moments. I am sure thoughts were on things dear—home and the life we had left behind and on dreams of what we hoped for the future. I am sure little thought was then given to our present plight, our lice, our sores, our frozen feet.

The drama and the pleasure of eating a D-bar as a POW emphasizes just how relative everything is. We have to compare each value and each experience with all others. This is why I feel I have been more richly blessed than anyone I know, because I was placed in a predicament from which there was no way to go but up. For forty-odd years, I have not lived a day without reflecting back on what life was once like. Not a meal is eaten that I do not reflect back on a time when there was nothing to eat. Not a day passes that I do not recall the time I could have lived off the table scraps from my mother's table. Not a night passes that I do not awaken to change positions to relieve some of the pain or cramp in my back or leg and remember how life once was. How grand it all is compared to what it once was, and this is why I feel so richly blessed by what occurred over forty-odd years ago. I can enjoy and appreciate so much that is taken for granted by so many. It is hard for me to understand why the Lord has been so good to me. I just have to thank Him for it every day in my own silent way. I hope that in some manner my loved ones have been able to sense this.

Work at the camp at Güstrow consisted of various menial chores. Germany suffered an energy crisis, and trucks were fueled by a wood-burning contraption on the truck body. One person fired the boiler or burner and one drove.

It was, therefore, necessary that pulpwood be provided. I still remember well one particular week in January when a group of us worked all day unloading pulpwood from rail cars. The weather was subfreezing and it sleeted and snowed most of the time. The siding was a considerable distance from camp, and we would depart as soon after daylight as the guard could oversee us. We worked all day, leaving enough time to walk back into camp before darkness fell.

Soup for lunch was carried to us in the field. Our guard on this mission was "One Eye." He had been wounded on the Russian front, and shrapnel had blown out one eye and a part of his forehead and face. All of our guards were rejects of a sort. One Eye no doubt had a psychosis, for his temper could not be anticipated. He could be docile one minute, then tear into an uncontrollable rage. He was then without reason.

On one noonday while unloading pulpwood, the prisoners drank all of the soup without realizing that One Eye was to have been fed from the same supply. When he realized what had happened, he went into a veritable rage. His behavior was maniacal, and for a while, we were threatened. In time, his temper cooled, and we made it through the day.

This was one of the few days on which soup was furnished us in the field. Needless to say, thereafter, we always determined if the guard was to share with us.

Work on the siding was just manual labor. The cars were laden with pulpwood, which we unloaded manually. It was covered with ice and snow and the weather was terrible.

The siding was next to a main line railroad and sugar beets had fallen from cars along the main line. We filled our pockets with sugar beets, anticipating that we would be able to convert them into an edible meal. I must confess that a sugar beet is inedible, regardless of the type of preparation and your hunger. We boiled them for hours on end and they never became tender. We tried to bake them or to cottage-fry them on top of the pot-bellied stove, but we never got a semblance of food from them. The residual from the boiled variety rendered a sickening clear liquid, which we drank. It may have had some nutritional qualities, but we could not consume enough at one time to receive any meaningful sustenance.

On other occasions, our work consisted of various chores around the construction yard. For several weeks, I was singled out to assist in making cinder blocks. These were blocks which were to be utilized in housing projects. A Frenchman mixed the cinders and cement with a shovel. He was Emille, and he had been in Germany for four or five years. Civilians from all over Europe had been brought into Germany for forced labor. They did not live under guard, and were paid in marks, and bought their own fare. I am sure they were under some form of surveillance, however. Emille had a little Hitler mustache which was the vogue. Most everyone wore a little black patch similar to Hitler's under his nose. Emille taught me a little German with his French accent. For instance, the German word for knife is *Messer*. Emille gave it a French version with a heavy accent on the last syllable.

Once Emille got a batch of mix prepared, I would proceed to place it in forms to solidify. The forms were wooden and held in place by metal braces. Two pieces of reinforcing steel were to be placed in each block to give strength. For some reason, the Germans counted the number of steel strands used to determine my work progress rather than the number of blocks which I finished. We were always looking for ways to foul up what we were doing without imperiling our well-being. Knowing that the Germans were counting steel strands rather than finished blocks I was able to make any number of inferior blocks. When not being watched, I placed steel strands in varying amounts from zero up to four. Not until the blocks crumbled on the building site would it be discovered that there was no consistency in their fabrication.

On some days, we had to rearrange supplies in the construction yard. Many were the brick which we had to handle manually in the snow and ice with numbed fingers.

I shall never forget one day when we were restacking some reinforcing steel rods. They had been lying on the ground and were covered with ice and mud. We had to break each one apart and then stack it in a new location. Fortunately, I had carried a sewing kit when captured and I had a needle and thread. I stripped a piece of the blanket to tie around my head, and I fashioned some mittens out of a part of my blanket. Even these mittens were not able to protect me when we were handling the steel rods. My fingers and feet became unbearably cold. The fingers were so cold that they ached. We were not too far from camp and, late in the morning, I decided I would walk off the job. I do not now remember who was guarding us. I had decided I was going to quit regardless of the circumstances. I ran the risk of being shot. I was hurting so that I decided to make the move regardless of the circumstances, and I just took off and did not look back. Down the road a piece, I was stopped by a German officer, and he returned me to the group. Nothing else ever came of it.

On another occasion, five of us were selected to work at night cutting wood into ten-inch blocks which could be burned by the civilians as fuel. We had the use of a power band saw that had five extra blades. During the day, the bands would be welded by a German civilian when they broke. He was not available at night, and we soon learned that as soon as the five bands were broken, our night's work was at an end. By letting the timber slip in the saw, it was easy to break the bands. We carefully monitored this operation, however, to get past midnight, so that we would not have to work the next day.

On this night job, we were guarded and supervised by a Polish gentleman. The story was that he was a count. He was a tall blonde and he had some class. His heart was not in it, and it was obvious that he was not concerned with our goofing off. We had a language barrier and I wish that I could have conversed with him. He was a nice guy who had been caught up in a turmoil that completely turned Europe upside down and inside out. He wore a long black coat with black boots and a black wool hat pulled snugly over his head. You could tell he was a "somebody." He was one to stand out in any crowd. We, of course, had to have lights while sawing wood at night. We were cutting the wood and measuring it in piles of cubic meters for sale. We were allowed a midnight snack on this job, and the Pole never rushed us with our snack. Another break on the night work occurred during air raids. Lights had to be cut off, and this, too, gave us a break from the work.

Another advantage of the night work was that we were

able to salvage potatoes in camp during daylight hours
when we were supposedly sleeping. Collaborators among
the forced labor groups from other European countries
would throw us potatoes. We learned that potatoes moved
to market on a road next to our north fence. These potatoes were in large open wagons, usually horse-drawn. A few
workers from varying backgrounds rode these wagons.
When we heard the wagons approaching us, we would line
up at our barbed wire fence and the laborers would throw
potatoes at us. These were scrawny little potatoes, no big-
ger than a golf ball, but you cannot imagine what a feast
they meant for us.

For a while, I worked under an old man from the
Ukraine. We consider this a part of Russia, but he would
not admit to being a Russian. In fact, all Europeans identified with the countries we knew before World War I.
Serbians were still Serbians and this old gentleman was a
"Ukranisch." His name was Andre Koch. He helped me
with the German language. He and his family lived across
the street from us in a pre-fab apartment unit. French,
Dutch, Russians and Estonians lived there as displaced
forced labor.

Andre was able to get me a table knife in exchange for
a measure of cigarettes. I learned that an onion was called
Zwiebel in German, and Andre was also able to get me
some onions. You cannot imagine how much a little onion
and salt can do to help a potato masquerade as a gourmet's
delight.

For a while, we were without salt. Cabbage soup without salt is a most unpalatable dish.

Willie Feine owned our construction company, and he
must have been a man of considerable means. After we had
been without salt for a considerable period, Feine obtained
a shipment of several hundred pounds of salt. They were

stacked on a horse-drawn trailer in one of the buildings near where we had cut wood and made cinder blocks. By a little hook and crook, we were able to steal one whole sack of salt and hide it in our barracks. We divided the salt up and hid it under the floor in cans. Until you have been denied it, you do not realize what a luxury salt is. Cabbage leaves swimming around in some discolored water with salt is not much of a soup, but without salt, it is an abominable hoax.

People have always wondered whether or not we were mistreated. We were not mistreated so much as neglected. Being denied shelter, food, clothing or medical attention can be as debilitating as mistreatment. I was never physically beaten by the Germans. I had a friend who lost some teeth from the butt of a German rifle. This was an isolated incident at this juncture. Surely the Germans could see their empire crumbling during the spring of 1945. They were being denied many of their comforts, simply because these comforts were not available.

Our medical attention was nonexistent. By the time we got to Güstrow, the open wounds of those who had survived had healed. We were then suffering from malnutrition, frozen feet, lice-infested sores, and general weakness. When one sees the punishment that these bodies can take and still remain intact, he must realize that they were put together by a Master Mechanic. The body has remarkable recuperative power and can withstand far more than we can imagine.

In Güstrow, a French doctor had been provided an office of sorts to look after the needs of all of the prisoners and the forced laborers from over Europe.

His office was in downtown Güstrow, and, I would guess, one or two miles from our camp. A sick detail would go there daily, but the main result was to get the day off from work. I had to go down for my frozen feet. They had become infected and I could not put my shoes on. The Germans got me a pair of wooden shower shoes, and I walked in these barefooted across frozen ground to the doctor's office. There was little he could do for me; however, on one occasion, he sprinkled some powder on my feet. On another occasion, he thought that three of my toenails were "ripe" enough so that he could pull them out by their roots. He pulled, but they would not come and I just experienced anguish. Our old German guard had been an English prisoner in World War I, and he learned enough to cuss a little in English. As the doctor tugged at my toenails, the guard laughed at me and cried, "Hurt little beet—son of beach." The doctor realized that he was going to have to anesthetize my toes before removing the nails, which he did. This was not an attempt on his part to be cruel to me, but the doctor simply was trying to conserve the few supplies that he had.

My feet soon healed over miraculously and I was back in the work gang.

It was on treks like this that we were able to forage food morsels from the streets and from the garbage cans of the Germans. Cabbage leaves would be retrieved from the street, and potato peelings were salvaged from garbage cans along the way. To say the least, the peelings were skimpy, because the Germans were on short rations themselves.

The only clothing issued to me was the old army overcoat from a war two or three generations before. This coat had to be from some old Prussian army. It must have been for dress purposes and not for combat, for it had chromium buttons down the front assembled in a double-breasted fashion. The coat was a heavy woolen coat and the color was a gaudy reddish brown. It did help protect me from the elements and I welcomed it. My socks soon wore out because there was no means of laundry and no change of socks. I was given two pieces of coarse cloth about the size of a large napkin to put on my feet as socks. You placed your foot in the center pointed to one corner and you folded over and across to form a makeshift sock.

While cutting the pulpwood for fuel, I was struck by a falling log. We were unloading pine poles six to eight inches in diameter and twelve to fifteen feet long. One end was thrown off the trailer and the other end kicked up and came back on my hip and back. I was knocked down and perhaps out. I do not remember. I was carried to our barracks and placed on my bunk. The French doctor was summoned and he got to me in an hour or so. Although I had on many layers of clothing, my flesh was torn where the edge of the log caught me. All he could do was sprinkle some powder on this wound. It was this lick that did my back in and later required disc surgery. Fortunately, I was sleeping on a board bunk, and this is the therapy that would have been required if the best medical facilities were available. After this incident, I was not subjected to any more hard labor, and, in fact, it was some time before I was made to go on a work detail.

It was also while recuperating from this ordeal that I was in a position to catch some of the potatoes from our friends.

The people I met intrigued me. So many spoke several foreign tongues. We had so much to say and so small a tool with which to converse. I had studied a little Latin in high school, Spanish in college, and I had just started German when I was drafted. All I knew were the vowel sounds. Fortunately, the Army had given us a handbook, which was of tremendous help. I learned to convey my desires for basic needs. I could count and pass the time of day, but I could not engage in an in-depth conversation. If only I could have engaged in a penetrating conversation with some of these people!

We discovered there are identifiable traits in nations as well as people, and I observed that human nature is pretty much the same the world over. People are born and die. They love and hate. They live day to day. They have the same frustrations. All seek comfort, happiness—a security. There is a yearning to live and people must do what is necessary to protect life. It is perhaps this animal instinct that causes wars.

I was given a platform from which I could observe people under trying circumstances. To observe and to be a part of the panic of warfare, of bombings, or survival itself was a glorious adventure. To have walked in the valley of the shadow and to have survived and to reflect on it for these forty-odd years has been a part of my sustenance. Life has meant so much more to me for having been there. I do not understand fully why so much good has been allowed to come my way. The good Lord gave me a strong body and a searching mind, and I just pray that He will use me in the way He has destined. I do not feel that I am cut out to be a witness in the ordinary sense, in that my relation with Him is very private. Yet, I feel that what I am writing here is being dictated by an uncontrollable force which has been welling up in me.

What the Lord did for me was to put me on the front row of a spot in history. Imagine being incarcerated with people from one end of the earth to the other. Practically every continent was represented there but Asia, Africa and South America. Every area of Europe but Spain was represented there. I even worked next to German political prisoners—both men and women. Some countries had been under Hitler for years. Poland and the low countries were first taken. They were the buffer between Europe and communism. I was impressed with them. They were strong on family and country, and I just had to admire this. I was astonished by the number of Americans who were first and second generation citizens going back to fight what their families had fled from.

Andrew Dora was the old man of my platoon. He came from Stamford, Connecticut. He was captured with me, and he and I were never separated after capture. He was in his forties and I, twenty-two. He could speak Slovak because his folks had come from one of the low countries. He was separated from his wife in his prime as were countless others. He held my hand and was a father to me. He talked of his wife so often and he was so true to her. We were separated at Fort Devans, Boston, Massachusetts, on our return, and I have not been able to find him since. He deserves a very special mention for what he did for my family. He was a real helpmate and a true friend to me.

And there was Andre from the Ukraine. He was as solid as an oak. His daughter was Ani, and her picture is in my album. I do not know their background, but it must have been of the earth. He reminded me of Big Papa. His hair was gray. He stood erectly and he was a man of character. When he talked with you, he let his eyes meet yours. Although we had a language barrier, we understood each other, and a lot of this was through the sense of sight. As old as he was, he had a twinkle in his eye. Andre wore one of those little quilted jackets that the Russians wore. I am sure it was a stock in trade for that part of the world. I will be forever grateful to him for getting me the knife and the *zwiebel*.

Two or three doors down from Andre lived another Russian. I do not know his name. He was a big burly guy, and he must have had a special trade because he did not

work with us. He had a very pretty daughter who must
have been around fourteen. He kept to himself and said
little. His thoughts, perhaps, ran deep. After we were liberated by the Russians, this man was out of it. He disappeared and the word was that the Russians got him because
he collaborated with the Germans. He would have been a
nice guy to know.

In addition to the French doctor, I worked with only
two Frenchmen, both of whom were named Emille. In
fact, every Frenchman in Germany must have been named
Emille. No one had a last name. One of the Emilles had
even grown a Hitler mustache to get in the Germans' good
graces. Their country had been occupied for five years.
Supposedly, the Emilles were not soldiers and were not
POWs. They were a part of the forced labor which the
Jerries brought in to muster. My impression was that they
were falling in line with the way of life of the Germans. If
the Germans had won, they would have capitalized on it.
The French had a great underground, but so many could
not be trusted. When we roared through their streets en
route to Germany, they were so happy, but some had
tainted the whole image by consorting with the Germans.
Even so, it would be great if I could run into one of the
Emilles now. I would like to know how their French-ac-
cented German is progressing.

As for our guards, we had all sorts, but most were re-
runs. I have mentioned One Eye and "Son of Beach." We
had one called "Pretty Boy." He had been wounded in
battle, and was still limping. He was a good-looking cuss, in
his twenties, I would guess. He was not with us very long,
and our guess was that he was sent back to the front to
fight once more. I had haphazardly played a harmonica in
junior high, and one night I asked him if he could get me a
harmonica. I had no idea what the German word for har-

monica was, so, mustering all of the German that I knew, I asked for a har-mon-i-ka, with heavy accent on all syllables. Apparently, I struck a cord, as he understood perfectly what I wanted. He congratulated me on my German, but there was no hope for a harmonica.

We had one old guard who was part of the Volkstrum. Volkstrum was a territorial army formed by the Germans in the latter part of World War II, made up of men and boys unfit for regular military service. He was the home guard, and, supposedly, he was too old for combat. He was a kind old man who held a rifle over my head so I would not escape. What his country and my country did not realize was that after the first three or four weeks, we could not have escaped and survived. In any event, this old unnamed gentleman held a gun over us. Yet, he had a sense of humor, and he was kind. He could have been a grandfather to any of our children. He was caught up in a confrontation in which he had no part, except perhaps a passive one. He enjoyed the same things in life which I sought: happiness, laughter, comfort, quiet, attention, respect, belief.

Yet, after we were liberated by the Russians and were free to do our own thing, this old man attempted to commit suicide. He gave us his rifle; he cut his wrists and he wanted to bleed to death. I helped patch his wrists and we sent him on his way. He traveled east across the city dump at which we had tried to trap crows for a meal. As he walked across the dump, I was looking out of the window from the guard's room with his rifle in my lap. Momentarily, I had the urge to take a shot at him, but fortunately, in a moment, the urge abated and I did not shoot at him. I imagine at that point our minds were still pretty clouded, boggled and confused. I still wonder what his fate was. I would like to have seen him again. He had a twinkle in his eye just as Andre did.

In fact, the twinkle in the eye is one of those blessings of life which the One Upstairs spreads worldwide. It is like the touch of a hand, the sound of a voice, the ripple of a brook, the laughter of little children, the silhouette of a tree, the whisper of the wind, the serenity of having been adopted and shown the true way.

The months of January, February and March of 1945 brought some of the bitterest winter weather that had penetrated the European continent in many decades. We still did not know what our destiny would be and whether we would survive or not. Yet, I felt most concerned about the plight of Mother and Daddy. It was while I was enduring these winter months in Güstrow that one of my December 9 notes from Stalag IIB would be received in Jackson. The second card written on December 9, 1944, reached the Jackson post office on the afternoon of Saturday, February 23, 1945, and in those days the post office had a heart. One of the men at the downtown post office recognized that this was a message from a prisoner of war. He called home to notify Mother and Daddy. They hopped in the car with Sue and the bird dog, Highstepper, to retrieve the first message from me since my letter of November 12. I am sure that the weekend of February 23 had to be one of the most joyous ones Mother and Daddy ever spent. They had suffered through the winter not knowing whether I was dead or alive, and to get this simple little note gave them the lift that they needed. This allowed Mother to resume her letter writing, and her first letter to me was February 24, 1944. Unfortunately, none of her letters were received by me and all but a few were lost, but some were returned to her. Hers, on February 24, said:

> Darling,
>   Your card written December 9 came last night.

We got it at 6:00 P.M. to be exact. We ran by Aunt
Mae's and while there talked to mama and papa.
Everybody is O.K. and continues to ask about you.
The Hyles, Longs and McCullens have grown to be
old friends, via telephone. The Longs called us
February 13 and the Hyles last night.

Harvey still stays by me. He has been busy con-
tacting friends. Dr. Fincher called me today. Things
are not as usual at Millsaps—not the same to you,
of course, because of new faces. Miss Bufkin ex-
tends greetings. She is the same good friend. Daddy
has hunted quite a bit this season. He said
Highstepper is the best dog yet. He hopes to hold
on to him. Ray was quite happy to hear about you.
Springtime is here. The jonquils, hollyhocks, haw-
thorn, japonicas and other earth flowers are in full
bloom. Our prayers are constantly with you. May
God continue to watch over you.

All my love,
Mother

Howard Hyle's family, the Longs and my family kept in
close contact, and after Mother and Pop received my first
card, a copy was forwarded to Washington. Mr. Hyle re-
sponded as follows:

Dear Mr. and Mrs. McCullen:

I am enclosing the card you so kindly loaned me
from your son, Dan. The Government photographed it and has made a record of Dan's location,
as they had no information whatever on him other
than the original notice he was missing in action.

We are enjoying the good news we have received
from Howard when we received his letter and card,

one dated the 23 December 1944 and the card dated
7 January 1945. He is in a prisoner-of-war camp
known as III-B somewhere in Germany, which the
War Department tells me is on the Oder River close
to Hanover, Germany, which is on the western front.
As you know the Oder River runs in eastern Germany and the town that Howard's camp was in has
been taken by the Russians and I understand the
Germans have moved these prisoners just a short
time before this was taken and therefore we don't
know where he has been moved. But anyhow, Mr.
and Mrs. McCullen, thank God our sons are still
alive, and now we can pray for their safe return to us.

I am enclosing a copy of a letter I received from
the Adjutant General's Office which is self-explana-
tory. This will tell you as well as Mr. and Mrs. Long
where our sons went into battle. If you can get a
map of Germany, we would appreciate it if you
could get us one. I have tried everywhere here to
get one, but so far have been unsuccessful. Also
would like for you good folks to keep in touch with
us as we will have a lot to do before this is over.

We will certainly have to get together when our
sons come home and have a real reunion and cel-
ebrate right, with many thanks for your kind cooperation and hoping to hear from you real soon.

Sincerely yours
Howard R. Hyle

The telegram from the War Department also followed:

Based on information received through the Provost Marshall general records of the War Department have been amended to show your son Pvt.

First Class Dan M. McCullen a prisoner of war of
the German government. Any further information
received will be furnished by the Provost Marshall
General.

    Ulio, The Adj. Gen.

As Mother was writing these letters during the winter, I
was still trudging along trying to survive under most ad-
verse circumstances. Each Red Cross parcel contained five
packages of cigarettes, and we soon learned in our own
Arbeit Kommando (work camp) at Willie Fiene's that we
could barter cigarettes for bread. Our daily bread ration
had been reduced from one loaf per day for each five men
down to one loaf for each seven men and finally one loaf
for each nine men. It was fortunate that I did not smoke,
and all of my cigarettes were converted into food.

    I was still most concerned about how Mother and
Daddy were making it, and I still had no knowledge of
whether they knew of my plight.

    As a result of the cigarette exchange, I have a fond
memory of another "pretty boy." He was from Holland and
he lived in the apartment unit across the street from our
camp. I do not know what his job was but he was an entre-
preneur. He could not wait to get home. The Dutch were
solid citizens. He was ingenious and he had a purpose in
life, I believe.

    On one of those days when I was recuperating either
from frozen feet or the back injury, the Dutchman had a
business deal. He wanted some American cigarettes and I
expressed a desire for some white bread. His term for
white bread was "cake."

    While we were sick, we were not well guarded and the
Dutchman suggested I come to his room. With trepidation,
I darted out of our compound into his little room. He

opened a footlocker full of items from the bakery. I had no idea that such delicacies were available. I chose a loaf of white bread. I am sure that it did not have the substance of the regular black bread, but it was a delicacy worth the risk.

This Dutchman was a manipulator. He, too, had been there as long as the Emilles, but he was willing to assume some responsibility with attendant risk. This perhaps is the great failing of our country—we dole out authority and goods and talk of rights without mentioning responsibility as a condition.

At some time during February or March, our German guards stole a cow and they butchered it in our kitchen. Our kitchen and supply room were in a separate building in the corner of our barbed wire enclosure. The kitchen had a tile floor and it made a pretty good facility for butchering the cow. The guards cut up and divided the cuts of meat among themselves and their families. I suppose they felt generous with our group of prisoners and the cow's head was given to our group. Our cook, Bruno, put the whole head in the soup pot and it seasoned our soup until it was nothing but a dry bone.

No doubt the guards could see the war was not going their way, and I suppose this was one reason they took the risk of stealing the cow. They also must have realized that in due course their plight could be much as ours was then. They obviously did not show the allegiance to their country that they should have.

Another incident also comes to mind to demonstrate the attitude of our guards. I was chosen as a part of the detail to go into downtown Güstrow to get our supply of bread. Son of Beach was the guard who escorted us to the bakery that day. We had some old tow sacks in which the bread was carried. The bread had no wrappers on the loaves, and it was handled pretty much as you would handle a stick of stove wood.

When we got to the bakery, we were taken back to the storeroom where the bread was stacked on open shelves. For some reason the baker left us unattended with Son of Beach and, as soon as we were alone, Son of Beach suggested we help ourselves to as many loaves as possible without making a count. We must have pilfered fifteen or twenty extra loaves of bread for our compound. We thought that we were really making a killing for ourselves, but when we returned to our lager (camp) old Son of Beach then blackmailed us for our precious cigarettes. He had to be the most distasteful German that I encountered that winter.

CHAPTER VI
Easter 1945

PERHAPS ONE OF THE most impressive moments in my life occurred on March 31, and April 1, 1945. At the time, I did not fully comprehend what was happening. That is why writing about these things some forty-odd years later makes some things blossom into even more important events.

On Saturday, the eve of Easter, March 31, 1945, we approached our guards and inquired whether we might be able to attend church services on Easter Sunday, April 1.

Our fate was still unknown. We lived from hour to hour, not knowing which might be the last. We were earnestly seeking admittance to the House of the Lord. We were cold and hungry, lice-infested and filthy, and certainly not dressed in Sunday attire. We were being strafed by the Russian tactical air force by day and subject to bombings by the British strategic air force by night and the American forces by day. We were yet to be caught in a no-man's land between the surging Russians from the east and the retreating Germans. Orders were given to have us executed. Life at that point was most perilous and we earnestly asked our captors if we could enjoy the privilege of going to Easter service.

We were denied this request, however, and were physically restrained from attending church by the armed might of our enemy. Yet, I enjoyed perhaps the most memorable

Easter I ever had either before or after that. To this day, I never enter a church pew that I do not reflect on my Easter of 1945.

On Easter morning, some sixty POWs in that encampment gathered in the larger of the two barracks for a prayer service. A little dim electric bulb hung from a single cord in the middle of the room. We pushed open our air raid windows, however, and the Lord had turned on His light with a brilliance we had not experienced that winter. As the sun shone through the windows, an eerie shadow was cast across the room by our prison bars. The only sound was the crunch of the black boots of our guard as he marched back and forth across the cinder path outside our window.

Here, these sixty-odd men gathered to hear the word of the Lord. Within the room were Catholic and Protestant, Gentile and Jew. None lacked the comforting hand of a merciful God.

The next to youngest man in camp got under that dim bulb with a little Testament and the rest of us hovered around him. John-Popa, a second-generation American from Ohio, whose family was originally from Romania, turned to the Gospel of Luke and started reading the undiluted Word of God. He read of the Crucified Christ and the Risen Lord. As he read, the tears slowly trickled down his flushed cheeks. Though his eyes watered with tears, his voice never faltered, his lips never stumbled. The Holy Spirit must have descended upon that room. A comforting hand was placed on each brow of every man there. Although we were to be subjected to much more in the weeks to come, every man in that room ultimately walked out of Germany a free man. (The only casualty of a bombing in that encampment was one of our guards who was blown into the little river nearby. That meant our bombardiers had to be on target to hit the guard and miss us.)

One point of this Easter story is that you can be denied access to the House of the Lord, but, if you seek Him, He will find you. He came into our little room and wrapped His arms all about us. He placed His hand on our foreheads and led us home. He sustained us when our hope was running out. I have forsaken Him and I have sinned against Him so often, yet, I have the comforting feeling that He watches over me.

CHAPTER VII

THE FINAL WEEKS

LITTLE DID WE REALIZE on Easter, 1945, that within the week all hell would break loose. On the following Saturday, April 7, our B-17 bombers hit the western portion of Güstrow. Our intelligence was right on target and an army installation was hit dead center by our own bombers. Fortunately, our lager was on the eastern side next to the city dump. Normally, we did not have to work on Saturday afternoons or Sundays, but after this bombing, we had no respite on either day. Our group of about sixty men was trucked out to the bombing scene almost immediately. One of our first sights was that of a man blown in half.

The army camp which was the target of the bombing was adjacent to the main railroad servicing Güstrow from east to west. The railroad had been severed in several locations by our deadly bombs. The Jerries had to restore the rail lines as soon as possible, and we were a part of the forces assigned to restoring the rail service. Prisoners actually were not supposed to work on any project which would promote the war effort. Rail service, of course, would promote the German war effort, and we were forced into this activity in violation of the Geneva Convention and against our will. There was little that we could do to protest, however, as we were under armed guards. In fact, we were concerned that the civilians might turn against us for the damage our bombers had done. We did not know but that the Germans might try to avenge their losses from our bombings by taking it out on us. The Germans, however, could probably see the handwriting on the wall, because they knew the Russians were closing in from the east and the Allies were pressing from the west.

Without any choice on our part, we were forced into a massive effort to get the railroad back into operation. There was a chaos of activity trying to fill the bomb craters so that the rails could be replaced. We worked alongside civilians and enslaved labor from all over Europe. Bomb shelters were scattered all over the area where we were working. Germans had been pinned alive in these shelters and a frantic effort was being made to free them. A number of our bombs were lying all about and there was no way to know which was a dud and which had a delayed firing pin. We never knew when one of these delayed firing pins would explode one of these bombs.

Notwithstanding the plight we found ourselves in, we did as much sabotage as we could and goofed off as much as Beetle Bailey. The filling of the bomb craters had to be done by hand tools, as there was no heavy equipment available. Many were the hand tools which we conveniently buried in the bomb craters.

By April, the German air force and air defenses were practically nonexistent, and our aircraft apparently covered the German sky without any flack or opposition. While we were in the middle of our work at the railroad on April 7, our bombers came back over to finish their mission. There was a pine forest to the south and everyone took to the woods, including prisoners, army personnel and civilians. When the bombers were in a position that a release of bombs would have been on target for us, we jumped into some of the earlier bomb craters and prayed. Fortunately, our intelligence information resulted in a direct hit on the first mission that afternoon, and it was not necessary for the second flight to release any bombs. There is no telling what would have happened to us either from the bombs or the Germans if the second flight had bombed us.

Being subjected to bombings by their own forces is to be expected by prisoners as well as front line troops. Having to live with the onslaught of your own forces every day and being confronted by the enemy was an ordeal. We were in the hands of the enemy and subject to their whims, and at the same time, we were secretly delighting in the success of the bombing raids. We were still quite apprehensive about our fate, because the Jerries could have gone berserk and killed all of us; no one would have ever known.

Our group worked in this bombed area off and on until the war was over. Dead Germans were removed from one of the adjacent bomb shelters for a week after the bombings. The delayed-fuse bombs still lay all around, and you never knew when another would activate. You simply had to resign yourself to your fate much as you had done in combat and be prepared to meet your Maker on a continuing basis.

After the rail line got back into operation, we were assigned to clearing some of the building sites and salvaging as much building material as possible. While engaged in this work one morning, we were attacked by the Russian tactical air force. It strafed us and the civilians back and forth, and I was able to hop back and forth over a brick wall and lie parallel with the wall to protect myself from the strafings. The brick wall on which I was working saved me on those attacks.

At this bombed army site, we discovered a large number of German army maps of this sector of Germany. We were able to steal a number of these maps and smuggle them back to our lager. We secreted these maps within the walls of our barracks and they later served as our means of charting our march back to our Western allies and out of Russian East Germany. The One Upstairs was placing little tidbits in our hands which ultimately would lead to our survival and our salvation.

It was also at this site that we learned where film was stored. After our liberation, we were able to appropriate a German camera and we helped ourselves to this army film to photograph the events of liberation.

After April 7, 1945, Güstrow had air raid warnings daily and nightly. The Americans flew by day and the English flew by night. I also noted in my little diary that there were frequent strafings by our P47s. This was a fighter plane which was widely used during this period.

We asked our guards if we could dig foxholes in our fenced area for protection at night. We were denied this request. We were locked in our barracks as the bombers flew over. We would pound on the door but it was to no avail because the guards kept us locked up. One of our guards was blown into the little stream which flowed nearby, and he was the only casualty which our camp suffered.

In the United States, at least in my hometown, our defense warning sirens blast at noon on the first day of each month. From the sound, our system is exactly like the system which Germany had incorporated. Thus, I get a little reminder of Güstrow on the first of every month—as if I needed it.

Fortunately, the German civilians never gave us any trouble during the bombing raids in Güstrow, although all of Germany was not like this. The timing no doubt had an effect, since surely they could see their downfall was near.

On one occasion in April, the situation was somewhat different. The air raid sirens started their incessant blowing. I was helping unload prefabricated material from a rail car to a warehouse. We were in the middle of a factory district which was a prime target. Everyone ran outside. It was a clear, cold, spring day. Everyone was running to the east trying to get out of the factory area. Our guards told us which direction to go and we ran with the others. We looked up and saw United States B-17 bombers approaching the city in perfect formation. No fighter planes appeared and there was no flack. The lead plane pulled the trigger. We could see the release of the eggs. Each plane followed suit and we could see the shower of bombs irretrievably released, with nowhere to go but around us.

We had learned that if you sight up your finger or up a pencil toward the bombs, you could see whether they were falling on your course or away. I sighted up my finger and found we were in the middle of the target. It was one of those times when you say a little prayer with a lot of meaning. You lie on your belly, but you get partially up on your elbows and knees to try to minimize concussion. I lay next to another GI whose name completely escapes me. We were just inches apart and I am sure both saying our prayers. Chaos was total. Our guard, One Eye, was behind us crouching to protect himself from the blast. While the bombs were falling, his rifle was fired between me and my friend. The bullet passed, barely missing both of us. It could have been accidental or deliberate. To say the least, it would have been a terrifying event were it not for greater dangers coming from above.

Men, women and children were all running frantically out of the factory district toward the east, hoping to avoid the falling bombs. One Eye's bullet ricocheted up the street amidst the fleeing civilians, but I don't know whether it struck anyone. The bombs would be coming in on top of us in a moment, and one rifle shot was the lesser of evils.

In seconds, the bombs started falling all around us and we lay motionless with a silent prayer on our lips. It was over in a minute and miraculously we survived the ordeal. Thus, we passed another milestone. Afterwards, One Eye was somewhat flustered. He knew that by firing his rifle at us he had done something he should not have. It all happened in a moment's time, but the memory of it has lingered all of these years.

It seems that everything which happened to me in combat and until my liberation was a near miss. To have encountered so many scrapes and to have come out unscathed is, to me, a miracle. The presence of death seemed to be forever with me.

We were always a little uneasy in the presence of the German civilians during an air attack, because we feared they would take out their revenge on us. One Eye regained his composure after the bombs hit, and he immediately assembled the prisoners entrusted to his care and got us out of the chaos which followed.

While we were leery of what the civilians might do to us in revenge, it seemed that those who survived the attack were just thankful to be alive.

We were beginning to see the crumbling of a world power from within, and this was quite a unique experience. The Germans had to sense their downfall during those April days. We obtained snatches of news by word of mouth and, occasionally, leaflets were airdropped. On the night of April 12, 1945, One Eye called us out of our barracks after dark to tell us that Roosevelt was dead. He was very solemn, and the news seemed to be alarming to the Germans. They must have thought that Roosevelt might be able to help their position with reference to the dividing of the spoils of victory with the Russians.

The Russians were surging through East Germany and

at that time probably were fighting for Berlin. After the battle of Berlin, the Russians turned north. We were located some 200 kilometers north of Berlin toward the Baltic Sea. It so happened that we were one of the last little pockets to be liberated. We were south of Wismar and east of the Elbe River. By some means, we had learned that the British and American troops were going to stop their attack at the Elbe River. This was one of the agreements made by Stalin, Roosevelt and Churchill at one of their summit conferences in Yalta. We clearly were overreached by the Russians in these negotiations, and this unwise division of Germany has led to so much controversy since that time.

Little did our troops know that they could have walked across Germany from the Elbe River and found almost open arms to greet them. Ironically, I later learned that my Eighty-Fourth Division would have been right on target to have liberated me if it had not stopped at the Elbe. Its course would have carried it directly into our area.

On Saturday, April 28, we worked as usual. Rumors were rampant regarding the progress of the war. We understood orders had been issued at some time prior to execute all prisoners. Rumors were that the SS troops were killing all prisoners as they retreated. We learned that the Russians reached Neubrandenburg on April 28, and that the city had been flattened on April 25 by our bombers and that Stalag IIA was burned. My prison photograph was retrieved at Stalag IIA by Melgary days before, and Melgary was able to hand-deliver the photo in France at Camp Lucky Strike. At about this time (April 28-29), we heard that Himmler was asking for peace.

On Monday, April 30, we were working as usual and had been moved back to the bombing site of April 7. A German soldier and his girlfriend ambled down the railroad and told us the war was over. With this news, our guards took us back to the barracks and this was the last forced work we did in Germany.

At that time, the German army was preparing defense for the battle of Güstrow. Artillery guns were being dug in and field telephones were being laid. We understood that Teterow, a nearby city, had been bombed and strafed, and that the Russians were within thirty kilometers of our city. We were technically free although our guards had not severed their command over us. We were actually caught up in a no-man's land between the Russian and German armies.

On that Monday, April 30, my former comrades, Squeak Williams, Vince Loguidice and House, came into our kommando (camp) after theirs had been bombed and strafed. They were running to the west hoping to reach the American lines and to avoid the SS troop executions which were rumored. Small arms fire between the Russians and Germans had already started at Güstrow, but Squeak and his buddies elected to try to make it to Schwerin, a city just to the west of Güstrow. Our group decided that we would sweat it out in our barracks at Güstrow. On that eve, our kommandant signed us over to ourselves. He prepared some sort of document which in effect released us from his custody as a German officer. We thought that the fighting would commence immediately at Güstrow, but for some reason, the Russian army abruptly turned north to go to Rostock on the Baltic Sea.

Our barracks were left open that night for the first time, and we set up a system of security on our own, taking turns standing watch.

On Tuesday, May 1, pandemonium reigned in Güstrow. We were technically free to do what we could on our own. Although the Germans were making a pretense of attempting to defend the city, the Germans actually were trying to flee to the American lines.

Our fate was still uncertain, not knowing how some fanatic German soldiers might react, but we knew that with a little luck and prayer our day of true liberation was near at hand. On Tuesday, we did some scouting around the city and learned of an army warehouse that was being plundered by one and all. We joined in and took some cases of canned meat, beer and other supplies back to our lager. There was some ersatz chocolate available, but even in our state, it was not palatable.

It is difficult to describe the chaos of such a situation. The Germans were at the very end of their rope. Their state had crumbled and they knew not what the future held. They were robbing from themselves and seemed little concerned about us.

One old German grandmother came up to me and threw her arms around me saying, *"Ich liebe die Amerikaner."* She then added another sentence or two. My German is not much, but she was saying, "I love the Americans. Why do you stop at the Elbe River? Why don't you march on in?"

I later learned why they feared the Russians so.

On the night of May 1, we again set up a security system so that we would know what was going on. Both Germans and Russians had combat patrols in the area.

On May 1, the Russian forces returned in strength from Rostock. Artillery began falling on the city. Small arms fire commenced. A few of us had spotted an underground caulk (lime) pit on the Feine construction yard. We elected to take cover in it because it was partially underground and it had metal doors as a cover.

We were hoping to hide there until the city was taken. We were still wary of what the Germans might do and were not sure that the Russians could recognize us. During the last two days of simulated freedom, we had fashioned a small American flag which we placed on our arms as arm bands. We had secured blue ink, sheets, and the like and made a fair facsimile of our flag for identification.

We then made one large flag out of a whole sheet. We tacked red stripes in place with nails, wire and odds and ends. The group that was going to hide in the caulk pit then crawled in at dark, and we spread the large flag so that it would be the first thing seen by anyone opening the doors.

Unfortunately, some Polish prisoners spotted us and came in. These were elderly political prisoners from Warsaw. They had taken part in the March uprising when they thought the Russians were about to free their city. This group numbered about five or six and we could not converse with them. It was our plan to let the passing armies go by above us and to maintain an absolute silence, hoping that we could go unnoticed. The Poles kept up a chatter the whole night; fortunately, things worked out. At daylight, we cautiously emerged from the pit to go to our lager. A Russian tank came down the road and told us we were free. They had taken over the city on the evening before, May 2.

Prison ID photo of Dan McCullen
taken Christmas week, 1944
at Stalag IIA

VE Day at Güstrow
Above: Dan McCullen
and Bruno Calka
Below: Kenneth Steier
and Dan McCullen
holding a loaf of the
infamous black bread.

Above: Andrew Dora with German revolver, and beer
Below, top row: Richard Rosa, Manuel Lopez,
Kenneth Steier, Dan McCullen; bottom row: POW Taylor, a
European girl brought into the camp as a laborer,
and Bruno Calka

Above: The site where I was strafed by Russian tactical air force in April 1945 while at work
Below: Mass grave for German civilians, Güstrow

CHAPTER VII

LIBERATION—
FREEDOM AT LAST

WE EMERGED from the caulk pit around daylight and cautiously returned to our barracks. I kept a very sparse diary and on Thursday, May 3, 1945, I recorded:

> After returning to the barracks, we learned that the city was taken the night before, on May 2. Free after one hundred and sixty-two days. Russians came to the barracks to tell us we are free. We go to town and people are looting all stores and homes. Stay in town most of the day. Everyone gets bicycles, cars and horses, and we tour the country. Willie Feine, our meister, swept the streets.
>
> This morning, it is still risky going too much; for snipers and small arms fire is still going on. We are finally off the soup diet.

To attempt to record now what my feelings were then is an impossibility. We had come through a six-month period during which we never knew whether we would survive. We flirted with death on a daily basis. The release of tension must have been great. It truly was a day of thanksgiving, and I know that I was filled with gratitude for having been spared. I was made to realize how little I really am. I

cannot begin to describe the feeling of humility and thanks
that overwhelmed me that morning. Nor can I adequately
describe the events which were happening about me.

I know that for the next several days things were very
unreal. In fact, the last six months had been very unreal.
We were caught up in a political struggle which involved a
hatred between the Russians and the Germans. The Russians were hell-bent on avenging the black earth policy
practiced by the Germans when they retreated from Russia
and through the Ukraine months before. As the Germans
had retreated from Russia, they supposedly burned everything in their wake. Russian officers described this to us,
and this was their excuse for treating the Germans as they
did for the next several days.

The Russians reminded me of descriptions of the Bar-
barians when they sacked Rome. The Russians came in and
took over the life of the city. They backed up American
trucks to the buildings and systematically looted every
block of liquid spirits, small radios, wrist watches and luxuries they obviously had never enjoyed. Some wore watches
from wrist to elbow. They would engage in gang sex on un-
willing, frightened and terrified German females. They
seemed hell-bent on degrading the Germans for the black
earth policy in the Ukraine. They raped mother and daughter alike. They were just out for revenge.

The Russian uniforms were anything but uniform.
Black boots were the fashion, but there was no uniformity
in the boots themselves. For the most part, it appeared that
these boots had been appropriated from German soldiers.
The Russian enlisted men wore either a little quilted jacket
or a slip-over tunic. The army lived off of the land, as there
was no quartermaster corps providing uniform provisions.
Every sort of conveyance and vehicle was utilized, and I
was amazed at the number of horse-drawn vehicles and

wagons which rolled into the city.

Women also were an integral part of the military complement. Even in the wake of battle, young ruddy-faced girls worked as military police directing traffic at intersections. Memorials were immediately erected in memory of the young Russians killed during the city's capture.

The army appeared to be an amalgamation of all ages, sizes and sexes. The enlisted men ranged in age up to the sixties. Some had Oriental features. There appeared to be little organization, yet they were well disciplined. We had fashioned little homemade American flags to be placed on our jackets as arm bands, and as we walked down the streets of Güstrow, we were constantly being saluted by the Russians. They had a respect for our flag at that time.

I have mixed emotions about the Russians when I recall seeing the German women bearing the brunt of their frustration. At the same time that the Russians were practicing physical abuse on the women, they were paying respect to us and our flag.

Our flag is never raised at a ball game and our national anthem is never played that I do not reflect on my six months as a prisoner. And while Old Glory flaps in the breeze and the anthem is played, chills tingle up and down my spine and tears still well up in my eyes.

Although Güstrow was still under attack on May 3, we reveled in our liberation. There was no law or order. Germans were running rampant. The German soldiers were shedding their uniforms, attempting to disguise themselves as civilians. Arms were discarded in rivers and streams. Residences and stores were abandoned. Looting was going on everywhere. I went into a downtown department store and could have taken anything I wanted. For some reason, I did not take anything. I do not know why I did not take

some socks, since I had been without them for months. I
suppose, in retrospect, we probably were in some sort of
shock and did not fully realize what was happening all
around us. We had been without a bath for months, yet we
did not avail ourselves of a bath when it was at our disposal.

I did indulge in one luxury, and that was a silk comforter which I took from an abandoned house. We elected
to stay in our barracks until plans could be made for our
journey to British and American lines. The silk comforter
did just great in my little bed of straw at the barracks.

For the next several days, we just bided our time getting used to the freedom of going and coming as we
pleased. Times were still perilous. Small arms fire persisted
for several days. Bodies lay in the streets and were run over
by vehicles like small animals on our highways. Sometimes,
the Russians butchered a cow in the street, and we could
get a piece of steak for our use. We were so far north that I
estimate we had only about six or seven hours of darkness.
For the next few days, I would sleep late, then have some
coffee and toasted black bread. In late afternoon, I would
french fry potatoes and cook some sort of steak. The town
bakery was reopened in a few days, and we could go to the
back door and get all of the black bread that we wanted.
The Germans were clamoring at the front door for a handout, and rations were rather skimpy. The confusion almost
resembled a mob scene, as the Germans pounded for their
bread rations.

On Saturday, May 5, I recorded in my diary:

> Dora and I stroll over the country all day. Just
> enjoyed being free to go where we like. Occasional
> shots were still being fired. The dead still lie in the
> streets, untouched, except by vehicle wheels.

Fortunately, we found a camera and we were able to obtain film from the military area which was bombed by our planes on April 7. We were able to capture a part of the next few days' experiences on film.

We were still living from rumor to rumor. It was difficult to get any information from the Russians. Language, of course, was a barrier, and confusion reigned supreme. The Nazis were hiding out and the Allies were trying to corral all of the Nazi leaders. Germans, civilians and military, were still trying to flee to the Elbe River and to the Americans. The Russians suggested that we might be returned home via Russia. We declined this option and elected to stay at our barracks. Other Americans gathered in the neighborhood, and we soon had two or three hundred liberated GIs who had assembled in the area.

On Sunday, May 6, I slept most of the day. There was no church that day, and VE Day was still two days away. I walked into town for a while, and it was rumored that we would probably move to American lines within two or three days. On Monday, May 7, I slept rather late and went into town around noon. I talked with an interpreter at the Russian headquarters, and the only instruction was to "sit tight." I returned to our lager around 4:00 P.M. and cooked steak, smothered in onions with french fries. I was still eating just about one meal a day except for the toast and coffee on arising. It did not take much to fill us up at that time, because our systems had been subjected to such a drastic diet routine for the last six months.

In late afternoon on May 7, I went to the German home of Herr Von Tongel. Von Tongel was a wealthy German who owned some kind of steel plant, as best I could determine. He had married an American citizen from Ogden, Utah. He had twin daughters in their late teens. One was a brunette and the other a blonde. Vera and

Norma spoke perfect English. Their mother had insisted
that the home language be English. These girls were as refreshing as any girl down the street. Their father had been
carried away by the Russians that afternoon late, and Mrs.
Von Tongel asked me to stay in their home that night. She
was concerned that her daughters might become the vic-
tims of the Russian oppression as had so many of their
neighbors. I had an enjoyable evening in an Americanized
home; they even had a record player with Bing Crosby
records.

When we retired for the night, the mother and both
daughters hid in the attic, and I slept on the den floor. I
was still in the same clothes in which I was captured, and,
of course, they were filthy and lice-ridden. Looking back on
this now makes me realize how confused I really must have
been. Here, I now had an opportunity to sleep in a bed and
to have a warm bath in a modern bathroom. It had been
months since we had bathed, and yet I slept on the den
floor without even taking off my lousy clothes. I did not
avail myself of a bath until I was in British hands.

May 8, 1945 was VE Day, but we did not learn of this
in Germany until some leaflets were airdropped. I slept
until 11:30 that morning at the Von Tongel home. I recorded:

> I had a good night's sleep last night in an
> Americanized German home. I got up at 11:30 and
> had fried eggs for breakfast. I went back to the bar-
> racks and Dora and Johnson and a few of us took
> pictures. We then went to the commissar's office
> and registered everyone. We will probably leave to-
> morrow. I also went out to the cemetery. The
> people are being thrown in large trenches. Entire
> families were wiping themselves out.

Liberation—Freedom at Last

> Later today I went back to the Von Tongel
> home. The father came in at dark after having all of
> the country home looted. I again slept here for the
> night.

The reference to the fried eggs was because it was most refreshing. I had not had an egg since November while in Holland, and to be served a fried egg in a private home was quite a treat.

In retrospect, my staying at the Tongels seems to be a strange turn of events. Why should I have been sleeping on the den of a German home to protect that family from our own allies? There I was protecting my recent captors from our own allies. The Von Tongels must have seen our bedraggled lot of prisoners pass their home daily while en route to the doctor's office or to another work detail. During those days of captivity, however, none of the German civilians tried to communicate with us. After liberation, however, any number of civilians engaged us in conversation. The worm had turned, and they looked to us as their hope for the future.

A lot of GI prisoners left Germany with a deep hatred for the Germans. The mistreatment and neglect which we experienced were inexcusable. Nevertheless, I did not feel any hatred for the Germans; otherwise I would not have engaged in protecting the Von Tongel family from the Russians.

The cemetery scene just referred to in my diary was quite depressing. I obtained photographs of some of the dead bodies being thrown into the long trenches. Grandfathers were pulling little goat wagons with the bodies of little granddaughters on them to the makeshift morgue.

Most had been hanged; their mouths were twisted and their tongues hanging out. Women of all ages were committing suicide. One pond was full of female bodies. Mass graves were dug and clothed bodies of all ages were stacked one on another for burial.

May 8 must have been a happy day back home. We had two enemies down and just one to go. Merriment must have been the order of the day, from all I have heard and read. Yet, for me, it was a somber experience to view the bodies of these small children and of women who could not face defeat. The German treatment of the Russians through the Ukraine must have been devastating for so many of the families to have wiped themselves out as they did. We obviously were still a very real part of a very real war, even though VE Day was being celebrated at home.

On May 9, I again had breakfast with the Von Tongels. I had again slept on the den floor as the mother and daughters hid in the attic. We were still biding our time until we would commence our trek to the west. At 2:00 P.M. on May 9, we learned that we were to begin our march to the British and American lines. We were still not certain of any details and we were never able to separate fact from fiction. We at first understood that we would hike thirty kilometers to the west and then catch a train. We were still hearing all kinds of rumors about the plight of Poland, and we had not been that far from Poland.

In any event, I returned to the Von Tongels to advise them of our departure the following morning. Their future was quite uncertain and the father even discussed the feasibility of shaving his daughters' hair and having them depart with us on foot. I then returned to the lager to pack enough provisions for about three days. We had no idea how long we would be en route. There was still no law or order. We just helped ourselves to whatever we needed.

On Thursday, May 10, we awakened around 4:00 A.M. Prisoners from all over had been congregating, and the group from our lager stayed together. We located a buggy and wagon and helped ourselves to two horses. This allowed us to have our supplies carried for us. Shortly after daybreak, around 400 GIs started on foot to march to the west. We were escorted by a Russian officer and his girl friend, who rode in a horse-drawn buggy. We were headed for Wismar on the Baltic Sea. As we walked through the streets of Güstrow for the last time, we passed the Von Tongel home, and I was able to have one last chat with them.

After the bombing on April 7, we had secreted army maps of this area of Germany, and we used these maps to plot our journey to Wismar. Wismar was being occupied by British troops.

The 400-odd GIs just stretched out up and down the highways. The northern German weather was cool and crisp, and the countryside was simply beautiful. Crops were being worked and everything was a fresh green. There were many lakes spotted along the way. We set our own pace. Most of us still wore the clothes in which we were captured.

Russians were running vehicles up and down the highway in a helter-skelter manner. Driving on highways must have been a newfound joy for them. They would push the accelerator to the floor, lean on the horn, and away they would go. In fact, it was not even safe to be on the highway with them. A truck struck one of our horses and we had to shoot the poor beast to get it out of its misery.

On the first day of travel, we covered about thirty kilometers. We stopped at a farm hamlet for the night. This was a large complex with barns, headquarters buildings, and the like grouped together. It reminded me of one of the building complexes on the plantations of our Mississippi delta. Typical farm scenes were all around us. Some farmers were plowing and some were on hay wagons. A pig was being butchered. The GIs bedded down in the stacks of hay in the large barns. Supper consisted of a little bread and rations from the sacks we had packed. We anticipated reaching British or American hands in one or two days.

On Friday, May 11, we started our second day's hike at 6:00 A.M. At about 4:00 P.M., we reached the outskirts of Wismar. The Russians had made no provision for us, and we did what we could on our own. We helped ourselves to water wherever we could find it. Comfort stations were simply the sides of the road. Our life for the last ten days or so had been that of a vagabond. When we stopped our travel for that second night, we located an old brick two-story school in which to bed down. This was our last night with the Russians. We slept on the floors of the school building. One of the GIs decided to look for some spirits to drink, and he thought that he would explore the attic to see if anything had been put away. A trap door was discovered in the ceiling and, once it was removed, we discovered seven bodies still hanging by ropes from the rafters. There were six girls and one baby in this mass suicide and murder. The baby had a birth certificate in its hands revealing that it had been born in February 1945. We elected to let these bodies hang, and went ahead and bedded down on the floors below.

On Saturday, May 12, we began the last leg of our trip into Wismar. We started around 7:00 A.M. The highway was filled with Italians and French who were headed home. We soon arrived in an outpost manned by clean-cut, Canadian troops. They were clean shaven and smartly dressed. Army trucks were immediately dispatched for our use. We were carried to a garrison home known as Eastland Barracks. We were immediately deloused and given some improvised clothing. After the clean-up, we were given a hot meal. Otherwise, we were still pretty much on our own. That evening, we went to a movie and saw "See Here, Private Hargrove." At the movie, we were able to see a British newsreel of the liberation of Stalag XIB. This was where we first had been housed in November and early December, 1944. This liberation was by the British, and I wonder now what my thoughts were on observing the liberation of such a hell-hole as Stalag XIB. I perhaps more fully realized our liberation on May 12 than I did on May 2. Just having a bath and clean clothes was such a change. We were being provided for rather than fending for ourselves under martial law or no law at all. For the first time since capture, we were furnished toilet articles, including a tooth brush. We were furnished three hot meals a day and we were served white bread for a change. I suppose the last meal of German black bread was the breakfast that morning in the old two-story schoolhouse adjacent to the Baltic Sea.

There had been no means by which we could communicate with our families while under Russian control, and we of course did not know if our families even knew we had survived combat and were alive. We spent much of the first few hours in British hands filling out forms and information for transmittal to our families. Although Red Cross communication was supposed to have priority to our families, things got bogged down, and Mom and Pop did not hear from me for several weeks. Most of the correspondence did reach them during the summer, although not in chronological order. Reviewing these letters now makes me realize how nervous and impatient I had become. My most welcomed luxury was the freedom to bathe as often as I wanted in a hot shower. In my letter to mother dated May 12, 1945, I commented that I had just had my fifth shower since October 1944. I don't know how we stood ourselves in that plight. We were still wearing some of the clothing in which we were captured, although the Canadians did give us a pullover white shirt and some underwear.

On Sunday, May 13, we were hustled onto some antiquated buses for a trip to Luneburg, the next leg of our westward journey home. As we pulled out of Wismar, we could observe the long lines of German civilians waiting for a handout of food and milk.

When we arrived at Luneburg, the Red Cross met us and got enough information to supposedly wire our families of our liberation. For some reason, this information was delayed and it ultimately reached Mom and Pop after some of my correspondence.

We were still under British command while in Luneburg and we just marked time awaiting flight accommodations for what we thought would be England. In fact, while in Wismar, it was rumored that we would be flown to either France or England within forty-eight hours. Armies apparently live and thrive on rumors, and we were living from one rumor to the next. We were still in a dream world, because freedom was so precious and meaningful. Having lived with death as a constant companion for the last six months, it must have been hard for us to comprehend our freedom and safety. There had been so many times that I thought that I would never make it, I guess that I was still pinching myself to be sure it wasn't a dream.

On Monday, May 14, some stripped down C-47s were flown to Luneburg, and my group was air lifted to Brussels, Belgium. We found ourselves still in Canadian hands while in Brussels. We were again deloused and we were furnished a complete Canadian uniform. We were advanced twenty dollars in liberation currency, which had been issued for money exchange following the liberation of these countries by the allies. Our twenty dollars was in francs, which could be circulated in France and Belgium.

When we first arrived in Brussels, rumors spread that we would be flying to England within two or three hours. This, of course, was an unfounded rumor which did not pan out. We spent the night in the Canadian barracks. I have no idea where they were located in Brussels. We were able to walk into the downtown commercial area that night, however, to observe the city night life. This was still within the first week since Germany's unconditional surrender on May 8. There was much merriment and the streets were overrun with thousands of civilians and soldiers of many nationalities celebrating the end of hostility.

A small group who had worked together as POWs in Güstrow still clung together. There still was no organization nor discipline. The Canadians simply provided for us in an informal manner. There was no routine or schedule and directions were given to us in an impromptu word-of-mouth fashion. After spending one night in the Canadian barracks of Brussels, we were shunted onto a passenger train which carried us to American forces located at Namur, Belgium. Upon reaching the American command at Namur, our carefree routine abruptly ended. We were then subjected to a semblance of a roll call with activities scheduled in normal Army routine. Namur had been a collecting point for POWs, and on the following morning, enough POWs had assembled to justify a train shipment to Camp Lucky Strike, Le Havre, France. Camp Lucky Strike was a large assembly point on the coast of France where thousands of ex-POWs were assembled to await transportation to either England or the States.

While waiting for transportation at Lucky Strike, we went through numerous interviews and briefings concerning our capture and treatment. We were put through extended medical examinations to detect any alarming conditions, and we were placed on easy-to-digest, soft, healthful

diets. We were not under any rigid Army routine for our
stay there, except to be present for the regular meal service. We were housed in tents and the overall accommodations were primitive but adequate. Compared to my last six
months' ordeal, I was living a luxurious life. There were no
duties to perform or schedules to keep. We spent all of the
day just resting or in idle chatter. We did manage to visit
around and it was amazing the number of our old L Company team which managed to get together. A number of
the guys had picked up an assortment of German knives
and handguns, and there was much bartering and trading
during the day.

Shower facilities for that many men were limited, and a
shower system was rigged up on a stream several miles
away. We hiked to the showers on a regular basis. We also
received the usual delousings at Lucky Strike, as we could
never reach the point that we thought we were free of the
creatures.

On May 19, 1945, I wrote Mother that our diet at
Lucky Strike was mostly milk, eggs and roast meats, with
no grease or seasonings.

I was a pretty pent up, nervous individual while waiting
for the transportation. We were still living on rumors as to
how we would travel or when we would travel. On May 29,
1945, I wrote Mother that I had signed up for a trip to England, thinking that I might chance a better deal home out
of England rather than France. An undated letter that I
wrote subsequent to May 29 revealed that orders were
changed, and we were to remain on the French Coast
awaiting a boat. Except for keeping appointments for
medical examinations and interviews, there were no duties
to perform. We were becoming accustomed to having three
balanced meals a day and our bodies were responding and
gaining weight. A popular USO show spent several days, or

perhaps weeks, at Lucky Strike and we would hike quite a distance every evening to enjoy this show. The one act which impressed me most was a song and dance routine in which Stubby Kaye sang "Don't Fence Me In." Stubby was a Mr. Five-by-Five comedian with a booming voice, and his version of "Don't Fence Me In" was a real hit with all of us who had been fenced in for so long. I don't know his background, but years later, I read about him being on Broadway and on the New York entertainment scene.

The morning hours at Lucky Strike were usually reserved for our physicals and interviews and briefings. Our service records were not with us, and the Army wanted details of our capture and the names of buddies who were killed or listed as missing in action. The Army was trying to put together all of the pieces, no doubt for its archives.

In the afternoon, we would either hike or hitch rides to the shower area and enjoy an open-air cold shower. Outside of the regular meals, probably the most welcomed luxury was the daily shower. We were still a nervous and frustrated lot, and I could not get it out of my mind that lice and other vermin were crawling over my body. Although the furlough to England did not develop, my election to detour through England just emphasizes how jumpy and ill at ease I was. One letter to Mother suggested that at one time I contemplated a return through Russia and the Middle East. I suspect that we all were a jumpy bundle of nerves, trying to cope with the fast turn of events since liberation day.

I was so uptight and restless that I sometimes would write a letter and then not mail it. I had been cooped up for so long and had been through so much that my actions were just abnormal. It would be a long time before things would return to a state of near normalcy. In some areas, nothing would ever be the same.

During the first week of June, I spotted a jeep from the 86th Blackhawk Division. This was a familiar division as it had trained in the vicinity of Alexandria, Louisiana, where my 84th Division trained. What drew my attention to that jeep, however, was that I knew my first cousin, Ira McCullen, had been shipped to the 86th Division about the time that I was sent overseas. The jeep driver was at Lucky Strike to pick up some film to be shown to the 86th Division, encamped nearby. I immediately stopped the driver and engaged him in conversation. He understood my plight of not having heard from home since October 1944. The driver stated that he could carry me directly to the company to which Ira had been assigned.

Since we had no organization or regular routine while at Lucky Strike, I simply got in the jeep and within an hour's time the driver deposited me at the company area of Ira's outfit. What a surprise it was to both of us when I found him in his officer's mess hall having supper. I partook of the officer's mess that evening and this was the first time for that luxury for this Pfc. I don't remember anything special about the meal except that we had some fresh sliced tomatoes.

I doubt if I ate much of anything, because I was so exhilarated by having found Ira in this setting. I still did not know what had happened to my family during the last nine months, and the anticipation of visiting with Ira was simply overwhelming.

Ira had just received fifteen letters from his home in Amory, Mississippi, and he also had received one of the recent Amory weekly newspapers, which told of my liberation. It had even published one of my letters to Mother about my recent liberation.

Ira and I left the mess hall and secluded ourselves on an embankment near his company area. We sat under the stars on a cool French evening, rehashing everything that had happened to us during the last several months. Ira was able to bring me up to date on everything at home, and I learned that everyone in the family was doing fine. They, of course, had been gravely concerned about me during the winter, but they had managed to weather the storm, so to speak. I learned that both of Dad's elderly parents were still alive. It was such a relief to learn that everyone was making out, and we were all looking forward to a state of normalcy.

Ira and I reminisced for two or three hours, as I told him what had happened to me and he told me about participating in attacks on the Germans at the Elbe River. His 86th Division was waiting on the French Coast for an early return to the States, as his unit was then scheduled to go to the Pacific Theatre for an encounter with the Japs. Fortunately for me, I did not anticipate that there would be any chance that I would be reassigned and wind up in the Pacific Theatre. Ira and I had quite an evening and we were still holding forth when the jeep driver stopped to pick me up and return me and the film to Lucky Strike.

On June 6, I wrote Mother that I had met Ira and I anticipated that we would probably be in the same convoy for our return home.

I made another trek through the French countryside a few days later to try to locate Ira, and I learned that his outfit had already departed for the States. The day was not lost, however, as I just enjoyed being myself and roaming at leisure over the rural French countryside. Army vehicles were about all there was on these rural byways and there was no trouble just hitching a ride from one hamlet to another. I wound up in one small village about meal time with a few francs left from the twenty-dollar advance the Canadians had given me in Brussels. I couldn't speak

French and couldn't find a cafe in the quaint village. I found a small pub, however, which dispensed delicious French wine by the glass for a mere pittance. The pub owner directed me to a nearby merchant who sold a small line of groceries. I was able to purchase a loaf of authentic French bread, and I had a delicious French meal of bread and wine. I doubt that the bread or the wine were that special, but in the environment in which I found myself, and compared to where I had recently been, I felt that I was dining with the goddesses. The memory of that French bread still stands out. The loaves were about a yard long and they were stashed away in the corner of the store, standing on end like sticks of wood. There was no hint of bread wrapping on the loaf, and they probably had been fly-spotted. Nevertheless, what a grand experience of being as free as the bird in the sky and enjoying the gourmet white bread.

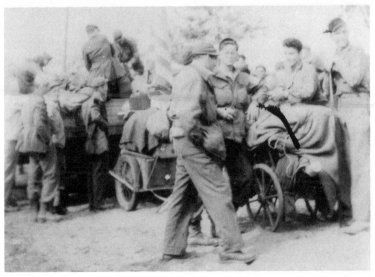

Above: Some of 400 American ex-POWs en rouite from
Güstrow to Bützow, May 10, 1945
Below: En route from Bützow to Wismar, May 11, 1945.
Those around the wagon include Morga,
John Popa, and Richard Rosa.

*Dan McCullen, en route to Wismar, May 10, 1945. The
satchel over the shoulder contained enough food for a
three-day hike through the country.*

*Above: One of the horses and wagons we stole to carry
our supplies while en route to Wismar.
Below: At Wismar, at the moment we transferred from
Russian to Canadian control.Standing: Richard Rosa,
Andrew Dora, James Johnson, Manuel Lopez, Bruno
Calka, unknown, unknown; kneeling: John Popa,
unknown Canadian, Dan McCullen*

After leaving the Russians at Wismar
Standing: John Popa, Dan McCullen, Bruno Calka, Rich-
ard Rosa; kneeling: unknown corporal, James Johnson
It was John Popa who read our Easter service.

CHAPTER IX

HOMECOMING

THE LETTER written on June 6 was the last letter written from Europe, but we did not leave on the 9th as anticipated. We finally boarded a ship and departed on June 14, 1945, and we docked in Boston on June 21. We came back the northern route in very choppy seas and wintry weather. We were able to sail this route without convoy, since the European war was over. We were hustled through Boston into Fort Devans. We spent two or three days in Fort Devans, still wearing the winter OD uniform that we had been issued in Europe. Of course, the weather was warming up in the States and these winter OD uniforms were pretty unbearable. In any event, they put a group of Southerners on a troop train within two or three days, and I ultimately arrived at Camp Shelby, Mississippi. It was necessary to go through more processing and there was a lot of duplication and interrogation, physicals, and so forth.

I was able to call home to alert Daddy about when I would be able to leave on my furlough. On the designated day, he arrived at Shelby during the morning and he was hale and hardy. We departed for home in early afternoon, driving a prewar car with recapped tires. The folks at home had been on food rationing, sugar rationing, gasoline rationing and tire rationing. At some point around Collins, we had a flat tire and Daddy put the spare on and we elected to proceed onto Jackson without trying to get the flat fixed. This was a mistake. When we got near Braxton, we had a second flat and it was necessary that we call Jackson to have a tire delivered to us. Mother was upset and disappointed because I had insisted that she not come to Shelby. For some reason, I wanted to first meet her in our living room where she had kept her long vigil. Aunt Mae and Bob and Wesley Ann were able to locate a tire and they brought it to Braxton for the change. After the tire was switched, we proceeded to Jackson. It was then getting late in the afternoon.

I do not think Mother ever quite got over the fact that Aunt Mae got to see me before she did. In any event, we pulled onto Warrior Trail, which is just one long tree-shaded block. I had taken a picture of just that scene with me to Europe. We parked out front. Mother had been sitting on the couch looking out the living room window, and she knew when we arrived. She maintained her seat and I strolled up the lawn and approached the steps. As I ascended the steps, she arose and, as I opened the door, she started across the room to meet me. Before we met, I remember that my first words were: "I thought for a while that I was not going to make it."

With that, we both choked up, embraced each other and nobody was able to speak for some time. It seemed the thing to do at the time, because I wanted to meet her where she had spent all of her time writing to me and praying for me, and on that very special occasion, a lot of dreams were fulfilled and many prayers answered.

We had a lot of catching up to do, and friends and neighbors soon started coming in. City Commissioner D.B. Sharron resided across the street and he was the first person to drop by. That evening, I am sure Mother had a very special meal with all of my favorites, but what it was I cannot remember. I feel certain that I probably had my first glass of buttermilk, one of my favorite beverages, since the summer of 1944. We stayed up that night and I related to them as well as I could what had happened to me, but in somewhat abbreviated fashion. After going through the sequence of events that had transpired during the recent past, I do not recall that they ever asked me anything else about it. I was as much concerned about what had happened to them as they were about what had happened to me and we spent the evening catching up.

My whole concern during my confinement was the welfare of my family and what effect my predicament would have on them, and, of course, their whole concern was about me. Although it was difficult to comprehend the things which were happening to us, I am sure none of us looked on those events as blessings. Yet, I feel that there is a master plan for all and that we are receiving blessings in disguise when we do not even realize it. Surely, our most recent events brought our family much closer together and much closer to God.

After spending a leisurely sixty-day furlough at home, I was transferred to Miami Beach for further physical examinations, processing, etc., and from there a trainload of ex-POWs shipped to Camp Stoneman, California, about forty miles across the Bay from San Francisco. We stayed at Camp Stoneman with no assignment until discharge in late November. Fortunately, Ralph (Squeak) Williams, who was my foxhole buddy in combat, was also at Stoneman, and we renewed our friendship and stayed together until discharge.

A review of letters written in September, October and November revealed the degree of frustration that we were under just sitting and doing nothing and speculating on when we might be discharged. I suppose we also were suffering from the aftermaths of POW camp, since we were extremely nervous and tense, and I developed a feeling of bugs crawling over me, which lasted for years.

On September 25, 1945, I wrote:

Dear Mother,

I'm just passing away the time doing nothing. I think I would be better off with a job or something to occupy myself with. I almost threatened to ask you to send my radio, but I will wait a while and see.

It is preposterous your thinking the army won't do anything about discharges on account of our physical condition. The medics here only laugh and throw me a bottle of liniment. One told me army medicine is socialized medicine and if ever I get a chance, to vote against it. He said as long as he is in the army he could do nothing for me. I guess I'm going nuts and it is no laughing matter. I feel lice crawling over me and I even went to be sprayed with DDT. Medical officers have inspected me closely and there is nothing the matter with me. It is all imagination and I can't do anything about it. It is driving me crazy and still it is my imagination. My nerves are so tense that I want to grasp something and just tear it to bits. It is too regular for me, eat and sleep day in and day out. If something does not happen, I'll go crazy.

Squeak and I sat on his barracks steps and talked to midnight last night, just talking about home or combat or the army.

Love,
Dan

•

How well I remember the imaginary sensation of lice crawling over my body. The feeling was as real as if the lice were actually present. I would scratch my skin incessantly even though I could not see the varmints. I remember vividly that one day as I walked down one of the streets at Camp Stoneman, I could feel these creatures crawling on my body, yet I could not spot them with my naked eyes. I thought that the best time to catch the little devils would be to report to the medics for an examination at the same time I was feeling the sensation. Therefore, one afternoon while at Stoneman, I reported in to the hospital in order that the medics could examine me under the spotlights. I was itching and scratching up a storm, and yet their examination was completely negative. I realize now that I was probably suffering from what would be diagnosed as a neurosis. This feeling of crawling bugs stuck with me for years, and I remember well all of the insecticides, flea powders and rinses that I dowsed on my body trying to suppress this feeling. It eventually receded, and now I only get a fleeting moment of that ill-feeling, like a short flashback. Nevertheless, the feeling of bugs still returns to me even today.

CHAPTER X

AFTERMATH

THOSE LETTERS from Camp Stoneman reflect some of the impatience, anxiety and frustration that I experienced as a part of the aftermath. From what I have read, and from studies made as late as 1981, it seems that these were common characteristics exhibited by most repatriated ex-POWs. I feel that I have been more fortunate than most. Studies have revealed that shortly after World War II an abnormally high rate of untimely deaths befell the ex-POWs. There was an unusually high rate of violent accidental deaths among former prisoners of war, including an abnormally high death rate resulting from single vehicle accidents. The suicide rate was much above average and violent deaths at an early age were frequent. One of the members of my platoon, captured with me on November 22, 1944, died in a gutter as a result of alcoholism. Another one of my platoon members and a good friend gunned down his girlfriend on a busy Miami Street corner at noon one day in the early 1950s, and he then shot himself to death at the scene.

Other studies still being conducted reveal that on the whole ex-prisoners age a little faster and die a little earlier than normal. There seems to be a prevalence of diseases afflicting the digestive system, the cardiovascular system and the nervous system. Dental and optical problems prevail. Nerves and emotions at times seem to go awry.

Looking back on those times shortly after my release from duty and my return to civilian life, I recognize what a change had come over me. I remember meeting one close prewar buddy upon his discharge from service in 1946, and he remarked, "Boy, Dan, you have really changed."

I did not think at the time that I had really changed, but I know now that there had to be drastic changes from what I once was. Every experience of life adds a new measure to your makeup, but the stresses and horrors of incarceration in a period of war had to have had a lasting effect. No matter how normal I appear and no matter how well I have adjusted, there is never a day without some lingering thought of the past. Sometimes it seems that it obsesses me. There is some part of every waking day that my mind lingers in memory of those days. A part of every night is consumed by the past and I lie on my pillow alone reliving the past and wondering about the future. My mind never seems to cease inquiring and searching and I still ask myself in those silent moments why it was that I was spared and not someone else.

Soon after I returned home, gasoline and food rationing were lifted. Daddy still had his prewar Pontiac because no cars were built during the war. Gasoline was dirt cheap by today's standards, and at night I would take the car and just ride and ride for hours on end. Mother and Daddy were understanding and they never asked any questions. The nights were sleepless and I am sure they often wondered where the mileage was spent and why the tank was empty. I suppose I, like the rest of the lot, was a bundle of restless energy and I was trying to put things together. The crawling bugs which I imagined were on my skin would harass me both day and night, but when it occurred at night I simply had to get out of the sheets.

I drove for hours on end. I just wanted to be alone to

try to think things through. Maybe this was what was happening to others in my lot and this could explain why so many ex-POWs met death in those single-vehicle accidents. Maybe we were just on the road an abnormally excessive amount of time.

And then when I did sleep I was awakened with nightmares of the past. Even until this day, I experience these dreams of the past, but they do not occur as frequently as they once did. I still vividly remember one dream that I experienced a few years ago. I was to be executed and the captors had strapped me in a death chair in the gas chamber. I was elated with my predicament because I realized that I was going to cross the river. I was headed home and I could not wait for the moment that they were to drop the lethal pill in the acid. I looked up at the witnesses to the execution, however, and there stood my wife and eldest daughter heartbroken and anguishing over my plight. I tried to placate them for I knew that I was going to meet my Maker momentarily, and I was anxiously awaiting the event. The pill hit the acid and a white cloud ascended from the vessel. I smiled and drew a deep breath expecting it to be my last, and I immediately awoke.

When I returned to Millsaps, I only knew that I did not want to pursue the medical career that I once wanted. I do not know whether I was making the right choices or whether I was just stumbling along, but I suspect the One Upstairs still had a handle on things. We have a lot of options confronting us daily, but if our attitude is right and our motives are honorable and we keep in touch, He will give a helping hand.

For whatever reason, I chose history as my major and I was able to get my B.A. degree in January 1947. Even then, I did not know what my ultimate career would be. I was still very nervous and impatient. I had been working part-time during the last calendar year, and upon graduation, I worked full-time in the same job, but I knew that it was just an interlude until I could make another decision. Then, about two months after my January graduation, something struck me out of the clear blue and I decided that I wanted to go to law school. I had not had any inkling of a law career during my undergraduate days, but something hit me like a bolt of lightning and sort of prodded me toward the law. I still had no intention of practicing law at that point, for I had always been somewhat bashful and I had never been one to stand on his feet and talk. It was more my nature at that point to more or less blend into the background. Nevertheless, I decided rather abruptly during March 1947, that I should enter Ole Miss Law School during its summer term. I immediately applied for the June term and was accepted.

Almost at the same time that I decided to go to law school, the Mississippi legislature was called into a special session. I applied for a job with the legislature for that special session thinking that this would be great experience for law school. I was fortunate enough to land a job as docket clerk in the house clerk's office, and as soon as the job was open, I accepted without even giving my current boss the routine notice to which he was entitled. Little did I realize that the experience which I gained with that special session would be of inestimable value to my law practice in years to come.

I went through law school at an accelerated rate, as did most GIs. A big chunk had been sliced out of our lives because of the war, and I covered the three-year course in a straight twenty-four-month period.

When I entered law school, I felt that the legal training would be an advantage in other business pursuits and service to the community. However, soon after entering law school, I realized that law was my calling. I was fascinated by the advocacy of law and I decided early in the course that I would have a hand at the practice of law.

1949 became a pivotal year as I hung out my shingle to practice law on June 1, 1949 and I married my wife Beth on November 6, 1949. Law practice was practically nil and money was nowhere to be had. The B-17 bomber crews in World War II used to say that they came back on a wing and a prayer and this was something like the way we got married. We had a lot of faith in ourselves and the future and a lot of faith upstairs where it counts.

CHAPTER XI

RECONSTRUCTING THE BITS AND THE PIECES

THERE HAS BEEN a continuing effort on my part and on the part of many others to try to piece together the bits and ends and to know and understand what happened to us on November 22, 1944. I have written many letters seeking information and many letters giving information. I have been to many reunions of my Railsplitter Division and at each reunion, I meet someone whom I had not seen since the war. We exchange stories and addresses, trying to assemble the bits and ends. It was through this means that I learned that only five men remained in my platoon after the twenty-second of November. Three of those five were subsequently killed and the other two were wounded in combat.

Not only have the Americans been trying to piece things together but also the Germans have been reconstructing the past. In the June 1, 1978 issue of the *Railsplitter*, a letter appeared from Hans Kramp of Linnich, West Germany. Our former enemy was preparing a reunion of the American and German units which opposed each other in the battle of the Roer Valley. The reunion was to center around Linnich during the fall of 1978. What was of more interest to me in Hans' letter was his inquiry about a group of American prisoners who were marched through Linnich on the night of November 22,

1944. I thought that this group was the one in which I found myself that November evening. I immediately wrote Hans the following letter:

June 5, 1978
Mr. Hans Kramp
Mahrstrasse 52
Linnich 5172, West Germany
Dear Mr. Kramp:

In the June 1 issue of the *Railsplitter*, a publication by the 84th Division, were excerpts of a letter from you regarding a planned reunion on the Roer.

What interested me was that one excerpt mentions a counter-attack by the 10th SS Panzer Division on the evening of November 22, 1944 on the road between Lindern to Linnich.

It so happens that I was in a group which was captured on November 22, 1944 in the Siegfried Line, and I feel that it is quite possible that it was my group to which you made reference.

My group consisted of 60-odd men who were remnants of the 1st and 3rd Platoon of Company L 333rd Regiment and remnants from a part of the 2nd Battalion of the 333rd Regiment. We were hit by a panzer unit as we were entering the village of Müllendorf. We were then marched through Würm and on to the East, and it is very likely that we were on the road from Lindern to Linnich. I would not have thought that there would have been an engagement where you mentioned on November 22, as it would appear that this was too far east for American lines to have advanced by that date.

Excerpts from your letter also make reference to information from a Mr. Joseph Coenen of

Lindern. I have checked back through my *Railsplitter* issues and unfortunately, I have not been able to find any correspondence from Mr. Coenen.

I would appreciate any information that you could give with reference to my comments, as it appears quite likely that I was in the group to which you make reference.

With kindest regards, I remain

Dan

Hans replied to me on June 30 but he did not mention whether I was in the group he alluded to. Nevertheless, he demonstrated the interest which the former enemy has in trying to preserve the history of 1944 in the Roer Valley. His letters and other enclosures follow.

The map on page 10 shows the path of the 84th Division; the short arrow is pointed to Müllendorf, the village where I was captured. The 84th Division actually had to circle back from the south and take Würm and Müllendorf from the east. I understand that this actually was not accomplished until after the Battle of the Bulge.

I have learned that our unit was counterattacked by the German 10 SS Panzer Division on the twenty-second. The commanding general of that unit was still living in 1978, and Hans gave him a copy of my letter. Hans sent me a little note on July 20, 1978, stating that the general was very interested in it.

In my letter to Hans, I referred to correspondence from a Joseph Coenen. I later discovered his letter in the *Railsplitter* issue of November 1, 1977. He is the pastor of a church in Lindern and he was still searching for a church flag which some GI apparently took as a souvenir. His letter follows:

November 1, 1977

Dear Mr. Keller:

I am in receipt of an old issue of *The Railsplitter*—the Veterans paper of the 84th Infantry Division. On one page I found the name of Lindern. I am very interested about War History, and I would ask you if you could give me some information about military actions and activities of the 84th Infantry Division: especially about I and K Companies of the 3rd Battalion, 335th Infantry, under Major Robert W. Wallace, during their attack against Lindern in the end of November, 1944. I would like to know what happened in and around Lindern, Beeck, Gereonsweiler area. This Battle must be terrible because all those villages was mostly destroyed. The tanks (Panzers) standing in the fields till 1949. One "Sherman" was standing in a Farm-House at Lindern, knocked out by a "Panzerfaust" and several German Tigers and Panthers was blown to pieces between Lindern and Gereonsweiler.

What happened to the dead Soldiers? Where are they buried? A lot of the Germans are buried at the cemetery in Wassenberg and Lovenich.

We are still missing a flag, which belongs to our Parish Church. The flag bears the words: "Sankt Johannes Schutzengesellschaft Lindern-1925." This flag disappeared during the War in Autumn/Winter 1944 at Lindern. Would you be so kind and ask your Comrades and Veterans of 84th Division if somebody has that flag? Maybe in *The Railsplitter.*

I also want to ask you, if you could send me one of the history books of the 84th Infantry Division (Copie?). I am also interested in some Photos, which were made in Lindern or other villages.

A few years ago I found an American Identify-Mark (Dog Tag) between Lindern and Gereons-weiler. It shows "Hughes, Merril P. 5563144 T 43 44 P." Could you find out who it belongs to? Maybe to one of your comrades of the 84th Division? Please let me know!

With Warmest Personal Regards—and looking forward to hearing from you, I am

Most Sincerely,

Joseph Coenen

Pastor-Pauli-Strasse 15

D 5131 Lindern, Germany

My letter to Hans in June 1978 apparently was still making rounds in Germany and on July 12, 1981, Franz Schmitz of Koblenz, West Germany, wrote as follows:

July 12, 1981

Dear Mr. McCullen,

In connection with your letter dated 6-5-78 to Mr. Hans Kramp, Linnich, I would like to write to you.

I have a copy of your letter and a translation, and from it I see that you were captured near the River Roer.

I was one of the soldiers of the 10th S.S. Division "Trundsberg." On November 29, 1944, approximately 7:30 to 8:30 A.M., we conducted a counter-offensive during which we captured approximately 80 American soldiers.

Maybe it is possible to establish contact with these former soldiers. I have noticed that you, Mr. McCullen, were not one of our prisoners. The dates do not match.

Our counter-offensive was on November 29, 1944. Among the prisoners were 3 officers, a Swede (immigrant) and a German-speaking American.

In case you know someone who matches my description, I would be very happy to receive a letter from him.

A problem is that I do not speak English. In October 1981, in Linnich, we will have our annual meeting (October 10-11). As far as I know now, 70 Americans will participate. Also, for the first time, some former British "enemies" will participate.

I would be very happy if you or one of your buddies could participate.

I remain with best regards, and I hope that we treated you correctly in those days. I further hope you hold no ill feelings toward us.

Your former enemy.

Franz Schmitz

I replied to Franz on July 21, 1981, as follows:

Mr. Franz Schmitz
Kruppstr. 38, 5400 Koblenz 32
West Deutschland
Dear Mr. Schmitz:

This is to acknowledge your letter regarding the October 1981 reunion in Germany. I am responding to your letter after having had a very limited translation. I hope to meet with another person in about one week to get your letter translated literally.

In any event, as I understand it, you were with the 10th SS Division on November 29, 1944, when approximately 80 Americans were taken prisoner. If this occurred on November 29, I would not have been in the unit.

I was captured at approximately the same time of night on November 22, 1944 in Müllendorf, which is just outside of Würm.

The letter which I wrote to Hans Kramp in 1978 had reference to a reunion in Linnich, which was held in October 1978. I do not know anyone who would have been involved in your encounter of November 29, 1944.

I hope to return to Germany within the next couple of years to retrace some of my old steps, and I want to travel through the area from Geilen-kirchen and through the Roer Valley.

Your letter alluded to the fact that you hoped that I fared well as a prisoner, and although the experience was anything but pleasant, I don't feel any animosity toward my capturers. I was transferred to eastern Germany and spent most of my time at Neubrandenburg and Güstrow, and I was liberated by the Russians on May 2, 1945. I don't know whether you can travel into East Germany or not, but I would hope to be able to get back to Güstrow and Neubrandenburg if I can get back at all.

Thank you very much for your letter and I hope that I have had it interpreted correctly.

Dan

As we were bitter enemies at that time, it appears somewhat strange that the Americans and the Germans would be communicating with each other now on friendly terms to try to piece together the bits and pieces of a bloody past. Something of a mass hysteria has to creep into a society to allow the politics to get out of control. It was the Germans who set out to conquer the world in 1939. None of our allies had any desire to expand their worldly domain, except perhaps for Russia, who had her eyes set on Eastern Europe. The rest of us were fighting to preserve freedom and decency the world over.

Hitler must have been a little bit of a maniac, and yet, a little bit of a genius to have hoodwinked the intelligent German people into such a prolonged debacle. Perhaps it is from this crazy, mixed up past that so many are now delving into that morass.

My thoughts dwelled so much on those times that I knew for me to satisfy my curiosity I would have to make a trip back to the battlefield and even into East Germany where I spent those grueling days of 1945.

With student guide Daniel Wienss, September 5, 1986

German historian Willi Offermann with Dan and Beth McCullen, September 8, 1986, at the site of our capture on November 22, 1944, precisely where Lt. Schupe and Rachofsky were killed. Shrapnel and bullet holes still show in the door.

Above: Sign marking the entrance to Müllendorf
Below: South entrance to Müllendorf and the barn complex
where we were captured on November 22, 1944
(Würm River is behind the camera)

Memorial south of Güstrow to the Russian soldiers killed on May 1 and May 2, 1945 in the Battle of Güstrow

CHAPTER XII

GERMANY REVISITED

I KNEW that there would be no problem in revisiting the battlefield east of Geilenkirchen. The question was whether or not I could revisit East Germany under the rule of the communist police state. When the International Ballet competition convened in Jackson, Mississippi, during the spring of 1986, I, by chance, met an East Berliner who was visiting in our fair city as a part of the ballet extravaganza. We met socially at a dinner party, and I immediately started inquiring about the feasibility of returning to East Germany to retrace my steps. I was informed that East Germany would be most happy to receive me, because it was in desperate need of western currency, and the tourist dollar was one means by which it accumulated western wealth. I also learned that the Palasthotel was a modern hotel in East Berlin where we could be accommodated comfortably. Having made that contact, I immediately decided that 1986 was the year for me to take my sabbatical leave and make my return trip to Europe.

We immediately started working on travel arrangements through our local travel agent, and our local travel agent had to work with the East Berlin Travel Agency, which was state owned. Reservations at the hotel had to be made in advance and payment had to be made before we could even arrange for visas. We spent most of the summer trying to make our arrangements, getting the passports, and getting everything finalized for our departure the day after Labor Day, 1986.

It was not without some misgivings that I contemplated taking my wife into an eastern bloc country, under Communist rule, and with little communication with this country. Terrorists were active in Europe and in the Middle East at that time, and I had some reservations about travel in that part of the world.

What possessed me to want to go back to Güstrow or to Neubrandenburg in East Germany is still somewhat puzzling. For one thing, the six months I had endured in that locale had completely obsessed my thoughts for some forty-one years. I think I had to revisit it to satisfy my own mind. Another aspect was that I might be able to establish some contact with Norma and Vera Van Tongel, whom I had protected from the Russian soldiers who liberated me in May, 1945. I had no idea whether Vera and Norma would be in Güstrow or whether I could establish a live trail to their whereabouts. In any event, reestablishing contact with Vera and Norma was another reason to continue with my efforts to revisit East Germany.

In spite of these fears, we both planned our journey back into the old world with great anticipation. We had complete physical examinations and our physicians had prepared a complete medical history for both of us, with letters of explanation for the various medications each of us were on. I only had a hypertensive problem but we did travel well prepared from a medical standpoint. Beth's doctor cautioned us more than once not to let Beth get dehydrated on the trip. This little caveat may have led us to the most remarkable event of the trip.

I had often dreamed about returning to Güstrow, but it is just about thirty kilometers south of Rostock on the Baltic Sea, and I had always thought that my best entry would be from the Scandinavian Peninsula, across the Baltic Sea into Rostock and down to Güstrow. For our 1986 trek, however, we arranged to fly to Atlanta and then catch a KLM Flight into Amsterdam. From Amsterdam, we would take the East German airline, Interflug, for our flight directly into the East Berlin Airport.

On Tuesday, September 2, 1986, we departed from Jackson, Mississippi, on a Delta flight in time to connect with a KLM flight, departing Atlanta at 5:55 P.M. The first good news about the KLM flight was that a mother and four children were boarding the plane and needed to sit with each other. In order to accommodate this family, KLM bumped Beth and me up to first class for the flight into Amsterdam. After a sleepless night, we arrived in Amsterdam at the international airport at 8:05 A.M. We would not connect with the East German flight until 11:00 A.M. While Beth and I were getting a breakfast snack at a snack bar in the airport, an attendant inquired if an abandoned briefcase on a seat near us was ours. We disowned the briefcase and the attendant then commented that it looked to him like it could have been a bomb. With terrorists continually on our minds, we hurriedly vacated that part of the airport to await our Interflug flight.

When our East German aircraft arrived at the gate, I began to realize that my trepidations about the trip were well founded. The plane was a Russian-made jet and it did not look to be the sportiest in the world. We had three flight attendants and at least three other crew members for the trip. This was our first encounter with East Germans and their uniform was a drab olive green which reminded me of the days of 1944-1945. We had been through customs on other occasions, but when we got ready to board the Interflug flight, they went through our carry-on luggage minutely. Beth had all of her medications with her to be sure that she would not be separated from those items should the luggage be lost. The East Germans had more than a passing interest in her medications, as they were probably concerned about the drug problem. This part of our search created no problem, however. Then, they took us into separate rooms and a lady frisked Beth, and I was frisked bodily to be sure that we had no arms or contraband before getting on the plane.

Seats were not assigned in the plane and we took two seats about mid portion of the plane. The tail section was filled with boisterous smokers and beer drinkers. The first class portion of the plane was simply four seats facing each other, with a table in the middle on which they could put their drinks or write or what have you. The first class portion of the plane was in the same section in which we sat. The seats were mostly wooden construction, with some cushioning on the seat and very limited upholstering on the back only. The seats were collapsible, and if no one was sitting in front of you, you could simply push the seat forward, and it would lie completely flat where you could stretch out your feet with ease.

Interflug would not fly over West Germany, and we therefore flew north from Amsterdam, across the North Sea, across Denmark and the Baltic Sea, and then down the western corridor of East Germany into East Berlin. We did receive a snack en route which consisted of some cold German black bread, reminiscent of 1945. The bread was spread with butter or margarine, and we were served slices of German sausage, salami and cheese. An assortment of juices and carbonated beverages was available but nothing such as a Coke. The crowd in the tail portion of the plane was smoking heavily and drinking beer and being a little bit noisy. In this setting, we sat very quietly and listened and observed.

Our flight into East Berlin was uneventful, except that the weather had become cloudy and it was a bit coolish. We landed at the Schoenfeld Airport in East Berlin sometime after 1:00 P.M., and it was drizzling rain and cold. I was amazed at the appearance of this so-called international airport. It was the gateway into the eastern bloc countries, and I would have thought they would have made it a showplace. It did not even have gates into the airport terminal where we could depart directly from the plane into the terminal. We parked out on the runway and had to walk in the rain to the terminal. Once we got inside the ground floor of the terminal, the first order of business was to go through customs. I was anticipating the worst. That being the situation, I opted to go to the men's room on the ground floor level before getting in the customs line. Much to my amazement, the men's room was completely inoperable. The entire facility was dull and drab and I simply returned to the customs line to not leave Beth unattended for too long a period of time. Surprisingly, we got through customs with no problem, and they did not even open our luggage.

We then went upstairs where I made a money exchange for some East German marks. I did attend the men's room on the second floor and it was operable, but I was not used to the female attendants working in and out of the men's rooms in the European terminals, with no thought of modesty. After getting some money exchanged, we then gathered our luggage which fortunately arrived with us, and we then were engaged in trying to arrange some sort of transportation to our hotel. There was no such thing as a red cap or other attendant. Thus far, everything was working as planned. I had been studying my German language anew, and I was able to make myself understood in a limited way.

We were able to hail a taxi cab and I was somewhat

taken back by its vintage. Although the airport appeared to be generations old compared to our current standards, the cab that we hailed had a vintage of about 1930 to 1932. It had an old stick shift in the middle of the floor between the front seat and dashboard, and it had the first, second and third forward shifts and a reverse shift just as our old 1932 vintage cars had. We had no trouble establishing our destination with our driver, and as we made our way into the inner city, he pointed out en route the East Berlin Wall about which we had all heard and read for the last twenty-seven years.

We were impressed with the appearance of the Palast-hotel Hotel. It was a modern structure covering an entire block, and the lobby and registration area were as modern as you would find anywhere. It, of course, was state owned but we understood it was being operated by a Swedish firm for the state. All of the employees were well groomed and dressed in brown skirts and suits, with orange trim. Most of the personnel could speak a little bit of English.

We presented our reservations only to learn that not everything was in order. They required a receipted voucher from the East German Travel Agency before they would accept our reservations, even though the room had been paid for in advance, and the hotel was aware that we were coming. In fact, they confirmed that we had reservations, but they would not accept us without the receipted voucher.

I was getting a little bit irritated and frustrated at that point, because the weather was becoming a little foreboding, and we had been without sleep thirty or forty odd hours. I did prevail upon the manager through my broken German and his broken English to allow us to place our luggage in the room before going to the travel agency to correct the voucher problem.

It was then that we learned that we had to surrender our passports to the police before we could get visas to travel out of East Berlin. We had already advised the Deutsche Democratic Republic (DDR) that we wanted to go to Güstrow, Neubrandenburg where Stalag IIA was located; Wittenburg, where Martin Luther nailed up his ninety-five theses; and to Potsdam, the site of the Big Four Conference after World War II. At that point, I would not surrender my passport as I thought the first order of business was to be sure that we were registered into the hotel and had a safe place to sleep for that night. Another cab was dispatched for our use, and the hotel had written out the name and address of our agency such that we should have no trouble locating the agency. Our cabby could speak absolutely no English but we were able to get to our destination without a hitch. The agency was located in a fairly modern office building, and fortunately, they had two attendants who were able to communicate in fairly good English. We were able to get our reservations receipted with no problem. We learned, however, that our visa into East Berlin got us only into East Berlin, and we had to go through more red tape through the hotel before getting a visa to go elsewhere in Germany. Also, it was understood that we had to be back in our hotel by 6:00 P.M. in the evening, and we were to stay there for the evening.

It was then getting late in the afternoon and the weather was drizzly and dreary and our spirits even more so. In fact, we were so despondent at that point that we even contemplated cutting the trip short and trying to get out of East Berlin as fast as we could and while everything was intact. Instead of trying to hail another taxi cab from the travel agency, we opted to walk back in the rain to just let our feelings hang out. I am sure the East Berliners must have wondered what kind of characters we were in that setting. We were bound to have looked dejected and tired while walking through the rain at that hour. We had to ask directions more than once to get back to the hotel, but we did get back before dark. Our reservations were accepted and we did have a place to bed down for the night.

I was again confronted with the fact that I had to surrender my passport. I had always been under the impression that while traveling in a foreign country you always keep your passport on your person. I, of course, had never traveled in a communist police state, and I was wary enough not to want to incur their wrath. I had already spent more time than I wanted to in a German prison. Therefore, after much arguing and with many reservations, I gave in and let the hotel manager have our passports. He stated that the police station was just five minutes away, and that he would have our passports back in hand early the next morning. The manager gave me a little adding machine tape to serve as evidence of my having given him my passports. Of course, this adding machine tape did not mean anything to me, and I doubt that it would have meant anything to anyone who would have stopped me.

Once we got into our room, we freshened up a bit in order to return to the manager to try to make plans for a guide with a car to take us to Neubrandenburg and Güstrow on Thursday, September 4.

I had created quite a commotion at the registration desk with the controversy about my voucher receipt and our passports. I also had cashed some American Express travelers checks at the desk, and the entire work force was well aware of my presence and from whence I came. I would deal with first one lady and then the other, and we would break off communication with our language barrier, and I wound up having some contact with probably five or six people on duty at the time.

The manager had assured me that it was a mere formality to have our passports stamped by the police department, but I was informed that I would need separate visas to go to Neubrandenburg, Güstrow and Wittenburg, as they were all in different provinces. I thought this too would be a mere routine, but it turned out not to be so.

At any rate, I then started trying to make plans for a guided trip to Güstrow as that was my principal destination. I inquired of one of the female clerks whether or not Stalag IIA would still be in existence at Neubrandenburg. When she realized that I had been incarcerated at Stalag IIA, she then understood why I was retracing my steps, and the minute she heard "Stalag IIA," she hid her face in shame. She obviously was embarrassed to have been connected with that part of the recent Germany history.

My negotiations with the hotel for transportation to Güstrow were making no headway. At one point, the manager indicated that a limousine would probably cost sixty marks per hour. In addition, I would need an interpreter, which would cost another twenty-five marks per hour. Then the manager suggested that he might take the day off the next day himself, and he would consider driving me to Güstrow for a price. It would only be about a two-hour drive to Güstrow and we would have no trouble in making a round trip in one day. Things were kind of left hanging in limbo Wednesday evening because the passports were out of hand, and the hotel could assure me nothing in the way of transportation or a guide.

Beth and I were fairly well worn out at that point, and we showered and changed clothes in preparation for the evening. We were impressed with the facilities of the hotel as it was most modern in every aspect. The elevators were commodious and music played in the elevators and throughout the hotel. You could hear classical music and grand American tunes by the likes of Gershwin and Cole Porter. We had a push-button color TV in our room, and during the morning hours, we could only get classical music, with no advertising. There were no talk shows and I would have to say their TV probably was an improvement over ours.

The room key was attached to a six-inch metal spike that would weigh at least a pound. In fact, it was the size of a railroad spike. You would not likely check out of that hotel without depositing the key. The room was quite comfortable with two double beds, but these beds were not at all like beds in the western world. They were built on the floor, with a wood rail around them and no springs. The bathroom was quite adequate, with a shower over the tub, but if you ran the water at too fast a rate, the tub leaked. There was an oversupply of linens, lotions, soap and the like. There was no hint of Kleenex, however.

An extra key on the door key ring opened a private bar in the room which was furnished with snacks, beer and liquors. We would not touch that with a ten-foot pole, because we had the room paid for, and I did not want to do anything that would upset my arrangement. The hotel even had ice machines down the hall made by Whirlpool.

A view from our window let us look across Lenin Square, and as dusk approached, the city became dark and the streets were completely abandoned.

The hotel had at least eight or nine restaurants and bars. The main dining room was just off the lobby, and we understood that you had to have reservations for dinner. We had not made reservations and we therefore became somewhat frustrated trying to get into one of the other inside establishments for a meal that evening. We finally sat in the lobby bar and sipped a German beer with a snack, and it was quite interesting to observe our neighbors.

There were Orientals and people from the Middle East and from all other eastern bloc countries, no doubt. I am sure that we were the only Americans present. After being turned down for reservations at several of the hotel restaurants, we were ultimately able to get into a short-order grill at street level in the hotel. We were able to get a small grilled steak, with delicious french fries. A salad came with the meal but their salads were always an assortment of cabbages or slaw.

On Thursday, September 4, we arose early and dressed for the day. The first order of business was to pick up our passports and we ran into a stumbling block again. We were given the runaround and we spent the day arguing with the manager about returning our passports. They were promised to us on more than one occasion, and he insisted that the police station was only five minutes away, but we went through the day without receiving our passports or any visa to leave East Berlin.

Our room rate included breakfast on the house so we went to the main dining room, where a smorgasbord breakfast was available. This would be our main meal of the day for our tour in Germany. One table was laden with various juices and drinks but no citrus. Plenty of coffee was available and the pastries were delicious. Dry cereals were also available, as was a smorgasbord of salami and sausage, along with some egg dishes. It was not the customary bacon and eggs made to order, which we were accustomed to, but we learned to make out quite well for that short duration.

After breakfast, we returned to the registration desk, making demands for our passports and inquiring about some sort of transportation to Güstrow. We were left completely frustrated on that Thursday morning, as there was nothing to do but walk the streets about East Berlin, remaining in sight of our hotel. We toured Lenin Square and

St. Marien's Cathedral, which was just across the street from the hotel and on the edge of Lenin Square. Although built as a Catholic cathedral, it became Protestant in 1539. It was quite impressive but it was still in a state of renovation, probably from the devastation of the World War II bombings.

Finding drinking water in any part of Europe is a real task. I never saw one water fountain in any of the buildings in East Berlin. Being cognizant of Beth's health problem and remembering our doctor's admonition not to let her become dehydrated, we lucked upon a small sidewalk *Biergarten* (beer garden) near our hotel. I ordered us two glasses of German beer and then attempted to sit at one of the tables just on the outside of the canopy. The proprietor stated that those tables were closed, and he more or less ordered us to sit at a table for four under the canopy which was occupied by a young blond German. Beth and I therefore sat down with this young German boy, who likewise was sipping a beer. We struck up a conversation through my broken German and his broken English. He had studied English for five years and he was a university student on break.

Our newly made friend was Daniel Wienss. I briefed Daniel on my background and the fact that I was trying to get to Güstrow, Germany to retrace my World War II steps and to see if I could find a trace of the German family I had protected when the Russians liberated me. To my amazement, Daniel stated that his father was an evangelical Lutheran minister, living in Güstrow. Daniel was the first person we met in East Berlin outside of hotel personnel, and out of 17 million East Germans, I wind up meeting Daniel with a direct tie to Güstrow. This had to be the Lord's handiwork.

Daniel was a student in electronic engineering at

Rostock University, just about thirty kilometers from Güstrow. Daniel's wife was a nurse who had just given birth to their first child, and she had come back to East Berlin to visit with her parents while Daniel was on a two-week school break from the university. Under the social system of East Germany, Daniel's wife would have one year maternity leave, with 70 percent pay coming to her. She was going to stay with her parents in East Berlin while Daniel was to go to Poland to work for two weeks during school break.

Our conversation became quite lively as we discussed the possibility that he might drive us to Güstrow. At that point, a table of Germans next to us became quite attentive to our conversation, and we did not know what might develop. Then, another rather brusque German in somewhat coarse attire joined our table and that made a foursome. Daniel and I still tried to keep on conversing but we both became more alarmed at the attention we were receiving from our newly acquired table mate and the table next to us. Beth and I therefore made a discreet exit from our table hoping that Daniel would soon follow and that we could contemplate returning to Güstrow with Daniel. Beth and I strolled casually down the street and just momentarily we were overtaken by Daniel. He obviously wanted to accommodate us but he was going to have to check with his wife and his in-laws, and he would have to postpone his train trip to Poland. We made our way back to our hotel, being careful to enter in a secluded entrance at the rear of the hotel. Daniel came to our room with us and we gave him our hotel room number and telephone number in order to start making plans for our return to Güstrow.

I then left Daniel in the room with Beth while I returned to the registration desk to see what progress was being made with my passport. Also, I wanted to inquire what progress was being made with a private guide and car. I informed the desk that I was contemplating making some private arrangements if possible to make my return trip to Güstrow. I left the registration desk and walked across the lobby only to be discreetly stopped by one of the desk clerks who had overheard me state that I was attempting to make private plans with a private driver. She obviously was concerned for my welfare and she cautioned me to be extremely careful what I did because I could find myself in trouble with the authorities. This was the first clue that I had received to suggest that not everyone in East Germany went along with the police state.

I returned to the room and Daniel agreed to call us sharply at 6:00 P.M. that evening to let us know definitely if he would be able to take us back to Güstrow. Daniel had his own mode of transportation, and he offered to take us just for the cost of the gasoline. In fact, he stated that it was his honor to do this for us.

With those plans having been made, Daniel then exited from the hotel in order to notify his family of his intentions and to cancel his train trip.

In the interim, I called our U.S. Embassy and talked with our consular general to inquire about my passport problem and to get his recommendations on whether I should return to Güstrow with Daniel. I had already let the embassy know that I was in East Berlin and to let them know of my registration and name in event something happened to me. The consular general stated that I would have no problem at all making this trip back to Güstrow with a private guide. I was cautioned to be back in the hotel at 6:00 P.M., however. He stated that there was nothing he could do about the passport problem, and apparently, this was just one of the inconveniences we had to encounter.

There was not much that we could do for the rest of

that day, except take walking tours in close proximity to the hotel, because our passports were still in limbo. We were able to look into some of the small food shops, where there were lines for the limited fresh meat and produce. We had a leisurely, early afternoon lunch in the main dining room, consisting of soup and sandwich, and reservations were made for us to have a good meal in that dining room that evening. The rain had ceased and the sun was out and the air was clear and brisk. Having met Daniel, my spirits were lifting and things were looking up.

On the evening of September 4, we had a lavish meal by East Berlin standards in the main dining room. An organist played dinner music for us and he toasted us with the "Battle Hymn of the Republic" and with Gershwin tunes all evening. We were able to get a glass of white wine with our meal in the main dining room. Otherwise, white wine was not available. Daniel had called us sharply at 6:00 P.M. to confirm that he would pick us up sharply at 8:30 A.M., Friday, September 5, for my return to Güstrow. I had talked a second time with our embassy, and everything was rosy and we were on top of the world.

Following our evening meal, we then went down to the lower basement nightclub where they had a live band, a very nice dance floor and bar and cocktail lounge. For some reason, no white wine was available in the cocktail lounge, but we did imbibe some red Hungarian wine that made the evening. The German band played very well and we had a blast dancing the evening away and in anticipating my return to Güstrow. Even so, my passport was still not in hand and we were to be confronted with another ordeal on Friday morning.

We arose early on Friday, September 5, in order to get dressed and to get a good smorgasbord breakfast before embarking on our trip north to Güstrow. I stopped at the desk at about 7:00 A.M. only to learn that my passport was still at the police station, just five minutes away. It was promised to me within thirty minutes. We ate breakfast and I then returned to the desk and still no passport. By this time, I was becoming quite irritated and probably a little belligerent. We returned to the room to finish dressing and to get ready for the trip, and Daniel knocked on the door before we were completely dressed. It was just 8:00 A.M. and he was thirty minutes ahead of schedule and still no passport. I called the embassy twice to try to get help, and at that early hour, the consular general had not arrived.

I returned to the desk and a tour bus of tourists was in process of loading up to leave. A gentleman from Britain was on that tour bus and his passport likewise had been re-tained. He was raising unshirted hell about his passport, and when I had company, the two of us pounded on the desk. Fortunately, our passports were delivered to us about twenty minutes until nine that morning, but they contained only the visa to Güstrow and no chance to get to any other sector of East Germany.

With our passports in hand, I then returned to the room, and Beth, Daniel and I departed the back way to get to his automobile parked on the street. I was surprised that a student would be able to afford an automobile, but Daniel's schooling in electronic engineering and his wife's position as a nurse no doubt put him in a preferred posi-tion. He advised that normally there was about a thirteen-year wait before you could get delivery of an automobile. His vehicle was second-hand, and the chassis was the 1962 vintage, which happened to be the same age as Daniel. The engine had been replaced or rebuilt in 1976 and the car ran very well. It was a medium-sized car, and the seat belts were so frayed that they were about to wear in two. Beth got in the back seat with her note pad, and I got in the passenger side next to Daniel. We buckled up and were at last en route to my destination of Güstrow.

We first traveled through some of the back streets of downtown Berlin to get to a main thoroughfare to take us to the *Autobahn* that ran from Berlin to Rostock. When traveling through some of the older sectors of the city, we noted that much construction and renovation were still underway, attempting to correct the bombing damage inflicted during 1945. Upon arriving at a service center on the northeast outskirts of Berlin, we filled with gasoline and I paid with East German marks. We then departed at about 9:30 A.M. for about a two-hour drive to Güstrow. The *Autobahn* was a four-lane highway, with a median separating the north and south lanes. It reminded me of our interstate system. The highway was very well constructed and in good repair. Surprisingly, there were a lot of vehicles, both on the streets in Berlin as well as on the highway, and I would not have thought that the East Germans would have been able to enjoy that much luxury.

We noted an abnormally high number of police vehicles on the highway, and there was also radar out. Periodically, we passed police towers along the rights-of-way, everpresent reminders of the police state.

The countryside was beautiful. For the most part, the land was rolling, with large level fields of black earth. It reminded me very much of the black prairie land that we see in northeast Mississippi, along the Tombigbee River. The land appeared to be very fertile, and it contained various grains, corn and sugar beets.

About halfway between Berlin and Rostock, there was a rest stop and service center, operated by the State. The rest facility was on the east side of the highway where we stopped. The rest room was attended by an elderly German lady. We had to pay for each item used, such as the urinal,

soap and a drying towel. There appeared to be quite a
shortage of paper and paper products. Immodesty pre-
vailed again as it apparently does in all of Europe, and the
elderly, female attendant had no hesitancy in patrolling in
and out of the men's rest room.

We then continued north, into the beautiful lake region
of northern Germany, with huge immaculate forests. This
was a good hunting area, and there were hunting clubs and
recreational facilities in these forests and at the lake sites.
We were informed that the hunting and recreational facilities were utilized by the higher echelon party members.
Hunts apparently were not available for the working class.

About twenty miles south of Güstrow, Daniel turned
west to drive us through Auld Schwerin, one of the old
settlements in northern Germany. The villages were quite
quaint and we ran into windmills that you would expect to
see only in Holland. Thatched roofs were common, as well
as cobblestone and brick streets. Domestic farm animals
surrounded all of the farm settlements, and I am sure the
farm families fared much better food-wise than did their
city brethren.

Daniel advised that during the 1960s and 1970s, the
Communist Party and powers that be consolidated the
farming operations into very large co-ops. They were attempting to cultivate on a mass scale, hopefully to improve
production. Daniel advised, however, that the large co-ops
were not as productive as anticipated, and beginning in the
1980s, they reverted to smaller productive units. This perhaps was an early signal to the East Germans that their socialist economic system was not what it was cracked up to
be.

As we drove along the rural back ways approaching
Güstrow, we passed through giant forests, and the Germans
were parked all along the highways and byways, picking

some type of wild edible plant which we believe was wild mushrooms. Shortly before entering Güstrow, Daniel stopped at a Russian War Memorial where I photographed graves of Russian soldiers who were killed in the Battle of Güstrow on May 1 and May 2, 1945. Daniel, no doubt, thought that I would appreciate seeing the War Memorial to the Russians who died giving me freedom.

Also, along with this back route, we would see entrances into Russian army camps where Russian soldiers were still occupying eastern Europe. It is estimated that there were approximately 500,000 Russian soldiers in East Germany. We noticed some Russian soldiers hitchhiking along the *Autobahn*.

Also, along with *Autobahn*, I noticed some other strange sights to the east of the highway, and I was informed that those towers were the location of underground control centers where utilities, service industries and defense activities could be operated underground, secure from atomic attack. Daniel seemed to be obsessed with a fear of nuclear war.

I did not realize in 1945 how quaint and unique Güstrow is. I still don't know all that I would like to know about it. In any event, it was established about 760 A.D. It has a population of about 35,000 people. It was a hospital city in 1945, and for that reason, it escaped some of the dreadful bombing that went on in 1945. In the inner city itself, the streets are brick or cobblestone, and they are quite narrow and winding. In fact, it is impossible to drive an automobile on some of these streets. As we approached the inner city, the railroad gate blocked our passage, and we had to await the passing of a train. It was this same rail line that carried me into Güstrow on January 4, 1945. As we awaited the lifting of the rail gate, I spotted two ladies whom I estimated would be at the right age to have remembered April 1945. Daniel and I approached them to inquire if by chance they were in Güstrow when the western edge of the city was bombed by our B-17s. These ladies remembered the bombing quite well. I then identified myself as a ex-prisoner of war who had worked in the Willie Feine Arbeit Kommando. Willie Feine owned the construction company where I worked, and he also was *Burgermeister* or Mayor of Güstrow. These ladies became quite excited to learn that I was an American and back in their city. They remembered Willie Feine and advised me that he was deceased. I had last seen him in 1945 when some of the liberated soldiers had him out sweeping the streets after our liberation.

These ladies also knew the Van Tongel family and we learned that Vera and her mother were living in the United States. Norma was living in West Germany and the father had died a few years previous.

These ladies were able to give us the name of a doctor in Güstrow whom they stated could give us addresses of Norma and Vera. Having Daniel available as an interpreter and as a native of the city was of inestimable value. I don't believe that we would have had the contacts that we did with a professional guide and interpreter. Daniel knew every crook and bend in those winding streets.

These ladies also directed us to the site of the Willie Feine Construction Company where our barracks were situated in 1945. My first order of business was therefore to return to this site and relive what had transpired forty-one years before. We then traveled through downtown Güstrow where I had marched as a prisoner en route to work. I recognized all of the streets and the little river that meandered through the city. Our barracks had been located about one block north of the river, and it was in this river that we deposited our raw sewage from our commando. As we drove toward the construction site, everything came back in focus with me, and I could recognize the terrain and where we were headed. It was along this route that I had walked in wooden sandals from my barracks to the office of the French doctor where he treated my frozen feet. That hike was along frozen ground, with snow and ice. I was only able to wear the wooden shower shoes that the Germans gave me, and I could remember vividly that part of Güstrow. One has to wonder why I would want to return to that scene and relive those days. It had become an indelible part of my being, however, and Beth and I will be forever thankful that we were able to make this return visit.

When we got to the actual construction site, there was little in place that I could recognize. A new construction company had built over most of the area, and there was no evidence of our barracks. The building where I had made the cinder blocks was gone. The brick home of the bookkeeper or office manager for Willie Feine was still present but it had been altered. A large group of men were working in the construction yard doing heavy, manual labor by hand, just as I had done as a prisoner. They all ceased working and started gazing at me, Daniel and Beth. I had an eerie feeling, not knowing what they thought of me and not knowing who I was. They were rather coarsely dressed in rough, durable outer wear which would protect them well in the elements. They appeared somewhat ominous and threatening to me, and with that uncomfortable feeling, I suggested to Daniel that we depart that scene and try to trace the Van Tongel family.

Our earlier female informants had given us the home address of the Van Tongels and we located that, but it was not the home where I had spent the night in May 1945. They had been displaced into a modest apartment type unit.

Daniel then started rapping on doors, attempting to find the residence of the doctor who could give us directions on locating Vera and Norma. Fortunately, the doctor's daughter was at home and she was very gracious. It was noon time and she had some part of the cabbage family on the stove cooking. The cabbage aroma filled her home. All of these residential units in Güstrow were the typical European, five-story flat. They remind you of the walk-up buildings which prevail in the New Orleans French Quarter. You see the same type construction in France and Brussels. The units are one room wide but five floors in height and usually with a basement. The living and cooking area is usually on the second and third floors.

The doctor's daughter could not give us the address of Vera and Norma. Her mother was on a holiday to the Baltic Sea, and she believed that her mother would have the address. She did give us the name of another Güstrow resident who might be able to assist, however, and through Daniel's knowledge of Güstrow, we soon located another gracious lady.

The next lady was a war widow who had been raised in Hamburg. Her husband was killed in World War II and she elected to stay in East Germany with his family. She was able to give us information about Norma and Vera but she did not have the address. I sensed that these people may have been leery of giving information to a stranger. It was interesting to learn, however, that these citizens received us very graciously and they showed no animosity whatsoever toward me as an American. In fact, they were elated to see an American in their midst. It appeared pretty obvious to me that they led a rather dull, drab life, with few luxuries.

It was well after lunch by this time and Daniel knew the location of the only restaurant in Güstrow. We had to park Daniel's car in downtown Güstrow and then walk through some of the alley ways and winding streets to get to a medieval castle. I had never seen this castle during POW days unless that happened to be the dungeon type facility where we received a hot shower during March 1945. In any event, the restaurant in Güstrow was located on the second floor of this medieval castle. I had no idea what its history was or how old it was, but it had to be centuries old. It was not in very good repair. It had formal gardens on one side, but even the gardens were in disarray.

The castle and restaurant were quite interesting. We had to walk up stairs to get into the restaurant area, and we had to sit at long, wooden tables. The lighting was very poor and I don't recall that we even had a menu. Beth and I had eaten the large smorgasbord breakfast before leaving the hotel, and I was so excited about being in Güstrow, that I really did not want much to eat. I got a glass of pineapple juice and a bowl of homemade tomato soup, which was quite good. I failed to order bread, however, and I did not remember that in this part of Germany you had to order everything you want or else you won't get it. They don't normally serve water with a meal nor do they serve bread or crackers as we do.

Daniel ate quite heartily. He probably had not had breakfast but he had brought a sack of apples out of his in-laws' yard, and we munched on apples as we drove up the *Autobahn*. Daniel ordered what appeared to be a flank steak or chopped steak, with mashed potatoes and green peas, and he ate with gusto.

After eating, we walked back to the vehicle to go to Daniel's home to meet his family.

Daniel pointed out the first school building in the Schwerin-Mecklenburg sector of Germany. Apparently, it was centuries old and indicated that the Germans early on wanted formal schooling.

In approaching Daniel's home, we again had to park the vehicle and amble up the winding streets to his mother's. It was located in another walk-up flat, five stories high, and just the width of a single room on each floor. The Weinss' living room was very modestly furnished.

Reverend Weinss had a telephone and a very elaborate radio system. There was no evidence of TV in any home we visited nor did we see any TV antennas. Daniel's mother was very gracious. Daniel's two sisters were also at home. The youngest appeared to be about twelve or thirteen years of age and she was still in school. The older sister was nineteen or twenty years of age and she was a physical therapist. All three of these children were blue-eyed, Nordic blonds. Although the elder sister could speak a little broken English as did Daniel, the mother could speak no English at all. I overheard Daniel telling his mother in German that he had met us in the beer garden the day before. I was a little surprised that he would let his family know that he attended a beer garden, because at that age, I would have withheld any information such as that from my mother, who was an avid teetotaler. When we returned to the *Autobahn* for our trip back to Berlin, I asked Daniel why he told his mother where we had met and what she and his father might have thought about the situation. He replied that his father thought there was good in everything but that alcohol had to be handled with tolerance and moderation.

After Daniel had his family visit, we then wished the family farewell as we had to be on our way to meet the 6:00 curfew in Berlin.

As we departed Güstrow, we drove by the cemetery where I had photographed the mass graves of the Germans who had committed suicide and murder on their families to escape the wrath of the Russian soldiers. We also passed near the site of the April 7, 1945, bombing, and at this site, a sugar factory had been constructed to process sugar out of sugar beets. The green forest to the south where we hid from additional bombing attacks was still present and green.

As we returned south on the *Autobahn*, we had to stop at the same service center again to fuel the car. On this occasion, we stopped at the gas pumps on the west side of the road, and we had to walk on a cross-over, over the *Autobahn* to get to the same rest room that we had shared earlier that day. When we returned to the service station, Beth got my camera and started taking photographs, and the first thing we knew the attendant in charge of the service center was raising his voice, and we were forbidden to take photographs. I thought for a minute that he was going to confiscate my camera, but he cooled off and nothing was done. This just gives you a little idea, however, of what a police state is about. There was nothing at all any different about that service pump than any other service station in this country, and why he would have objected to our taking a photograph, I have no idea.

They did have what we would term a convenience store, and all we could get was some sort of soda pop which resembled the strawberry and big orange that I remember as a young child during the Depression days. There was nothing there to resemble a Coca-Cola, a Pepsi or a Sprite.

We arrived back at our hotel in plenty of time to meet our 6:00 P.M. curfew. We were careful to make sure that Daniel had our addresses and that we had his address and his family's address, as it was our intention to try to keep in contact and particularly to try to locate Vera and Norma Van Tongel. As we departed, Beth remarked to Daniel that the Lord had brought us together. With that comment, Daniel choked up and could not say anything. He was obviously moved. I then handed him a crisp one hundred dollar bill in U.S. currency which would have been the equivalent of about one half month's work. I knew that he could trade it on the black market and probably get several times its value. He was most appreciative of our generosity, and I, of course, was most pleased with the turn of events that day.

I don't think there is any question but that it was the handiwork of the Lord that placed us at that same table with Daniel in the sidewalk cafe on Thursday, September 4. I don't know how else to explain that out of the 17 million East Germans, we would wind up sitting at a table with this one blond German who just happened to be from Güstrow and the son of a evangelical minister. That night, Beth and I repacked our bags as we were to fly back to Amsterdam on an 8:00 A.M. flight by Interflug the following morning. That portion of our trip was most rewarding, even if we had been aborted in making the trip to Wittenburg and to Neubrandenburg. Wittenburg is a little north and west of Berlin and would not have been too far out of our way if we had had the time. It was at Wittenburg that Martin Luther nailed up his ninety-five theses and started the Protestant Reformation. The church in Güstrow was a twelfth-century church which obviously would have been Catholic initially, but it had become Lutheran after the reformation. So had St. Marien's Church in East Berlin.

We arose early the next morning and we skipped breakfast in order to get an early cab to the airport to be sure that everything was in order for our flight to Amsterdam. Again, we noticed the deplorable condition of the air terminal. There were no newspapers available except one which was stuck in a wooden container similar to those used in our public libraries. We boarded the flight on time and flew back in the same type of dilapidated plane that we had flown in four days earlier. Breakfast consisted of black German bread, spread with butter or margarine and cold sausage, salami and cheese, served with a little red Italian Chianti wine. To say the least, it was not the type breakfast that we were normally used to.

After deplaning in Amsterdam, we caught a commuter flight into Brussels, Belgium, where we were registered at the Sheraton. Needless to say, the cost differential was noticeable. The room rate at the Sheraton was 9600 Belgium francs or about $200 per day. We were in the downtown area, however, in easy walking distance of the shopping and business district, and the most welcome sight on Saturday, September 6, was walking down the main street and seeing the big M arch denoting the presence of a McDonald's. We went immediately and partook of a McDonald's hamburger, french fries and Coca-Cola. Things were returning to normal.

On Monday, September 8, we had arranged for a limousine, with a driver experienced in many languages, to carry us back into the Siegfried Line. Our guide appeared promptly in a new Mercedes and we left to retrace the battle scene of November, 1944. The scene had completely changed but the Würm River still flowed gently through Suggerath and Müllendorf, and we had no trouble in locating the exact site of my capture. This also was the exact site where Lieutenant Schupe and our radio man, Robert Rachofsky, were killed on the evening of November 22. A German history buff appeared on the scene as we inspected that site, and he confirmed the fact that I had been captured there. He knew my company commander and we went back to his home where he even had my division decal on his den wall. He had hundreds of photographs of the war scene in 1944, but with the press of time, we had no opportunity to visit with him. I did learn that a friend of mine who had been incarcerated with me at Güstrow had returned to the battle scene and had visited in the home of this German. My friend is from Raleigh, North Carolina, and I have not yet been able to run him down. We have not seen each other since Ft. Devans, Massachusetts, after our return to the States in June 1945.

What is so astonishing to me is that there is so much interest being generated now regarding events which occurred two generations ago. What is even more astonishing, however, is the fact that the world has grown so much smaller, and you can cross paths with people who have mutual interest and acquaintances.

The tour of the battlefield was somewhat anticlimatic after having spent four days in East Germany and in Güstrow. I am sure, however, that it was quite meaningful to Beth. She was seeing the serene landscape as it exists today, and I was trying to visualize how it appeared in 1944. The old trestle under the railroad was still in a state of despair much as it had been in 1944. Homes had been rebuilt and refurbished and few buildings showed the scars of the battle. All pillboxes had been destroyed and I could only guess where they had been. The peace and serenity of the countryside was difficult for me to put in focus compared to the chaos and destruction which had existed in 1944. Be that as it may, my overall postwar trip to Germany was exciting and fulfilling.

EPILOGUE

After having returned home and reflected on the trip to East Germany, I realized more and more that revelations coming out of that trip are more than just the satisfaction of my own curiosity. If I had not met Daniel when I did at the sidewalk cafe, there would have been no way that my hotel would have arranged a trip back to Güstrow. I am convinced that this meeting was the handiwork of the Living God, as it was His hand which led me through the battle and through liberation.

Daniel persisted in his efforts to trace Vera and Norma Van Tongel. Eventually I received an updated address for Vera, who now lives in Sacramento, California, and learned that Norma is teaching education to the handicapped in Stuttgart. Daniel advised that one of my letters had made its way to his father's home, but it had been opened and presumably the contents copied. I was worried that I may be putting Daniel in jeopardy.

I made contact with Vera and we have exchanged letters on more than one occasion. She suggested that I cease writing Daniel for the time being, because it was suspected that I was an agent and that Daniel could be in jeopardy. Since that time the Berlin Wall has crumbled and the eastern bloc countries have been doing their own thing. With more communications developing between these countries, I am anticipating a renewed contact from Daniel.

Daniel has learned well the teaching of the socialist

system in East Germany. He relates capitalism with aggression and war. Daniel is seeking peace on this earth, and I really do believe that he is a true Christian.

Although I associated with the Russians on a very limited basis, I could relate to them individually just as I did with some of the Germans after my liberation. I could relate with Daniel also, but it is obvious that our political views are miles apart. It is good that we could meet one on one, however, and if we could have one-on-one diplomacy and one-on-one communication, wars would cease. We all experience the same feelings, and I am sure that on an individual basis everyone loves peace and tranquility and wants to experience a meaningful and happy life while on this planet.